A TOWN CALLED TOILETS

A TOWN CALLED TOILETS
THE CONFESSIONS OF A SHETLAND TOUR GUIDE

ALLEN FRASER

The Shetland Times Ltd
Lerwick
2018

A Town Called Toilets: The Confessions of a Shetland Tour Guide

Copyright © Allen Fraser, 2018.

Allen Fraser has asserted his right to be identified as the author of this work in accordance with the Copyright, Design and Patents Act 1988.

ISBN 978-1-910997-19-2

A catalogue record for this book is available from the British Library.

All rights reserved.
No part of this publication may be reproduced, stored in a retrieval system, or transmitted, in any form, by any means, electronic, mechanical, photocopying, recording or otherwise, without the prior written permission of the publishers.

Printed and published by
The Shetland Times Ltd.,
Gremista, Lerwick,
Shetland ZE1 0PX.

This book is dedicated to my wife, Ann, and to the memory of my late parents, Walter Fraser and Ann Urquhart.

ACKNOWLEDGEMENTS

My thanks to Jenny Murray for proof reading the first draft this book and for her encouraging comments. Thanks also to Shetland Museum and Archives, Rory Gillies Shetland Flyer Aerial Media, David Gifford Photography, Cullivoe Up-Helly-A' Committee and Sunniva Leask, Bill Urquhart, Ian Smith, Catherine Jamieson and Eileen Mullay in providing additional photographs used in this book.

Grateful thanks to Astrid Hess for information on the life of her great-aunt Nellie Smith and for permission to use photos of Nellie and the Smith family and to reproduce Nellie's poem *Dear Auld Hame*; also to the family of the late Rhoda Bulter for permission to reproduce a verse from her poem *Shetlandic*.

CONTENTS

Prologue xi

PHASE ONE

    Fit the First: Yell 3
        'Hame-aboot' 3
        Growing up with grand-folk 6
        Parents 8

    Fit the Second: This Crofting Life 17
        All change 17
        Growing the croft 18
        'Paet' and 'haet' 26
        A cordial visit 28
        A 'caa' and 'clootie-dugs' 28
        Collies and 'kollies' 29
        'Twallin' kye and six score draws 32
        Onybody spoken fur de 'faa'? 33

    Fit the Third: Pastimes and Past Times 35
        Staples 36
        'Eela' 37
        'Ebb' 40
        'Trootin' 42
        Regatta days 43
        At da hall 44
        Da 'picters' and da 'wireless' 47
        'Atween' da 'brods' 49
        Sent-errands and star-struck 50
        'Haddin oot a langer' 53
        'Reddin' up kin 53

    Fit the Fourth: Educating Allen 55
        Gutcher schooldays 55
        The long hot summer 58
        Mid Yell schooldays 59
        Lerwick Central School 61
        Granite City 62
        The deer hunter 64
        Brief encounter 65
        Pride before a fail 66
        A change of course. 68

    Fit the Fifth: A Semester in the University of Life 71
        'Wirkin' at da fish 71
        Dem dry bones 75
        So long, and thanks for all the fish 76
        Full circle 77

(Continued overleaf)

PHASE TWO

Fit the Sixth: On the Rocks 83
    Over the moon 83
    A tour guide is born 84
    Geopark Shetland 86
    Shetland Geotours 88

Fit the Seventh: Sights, Sites and Sightings 90
    Visitors' vistas 91
    Weather 94
    Safety first 96
    Centres of attraction 100
    Shaggy dog story 103
    Stranger on the shore 104
    Ley line seeker 105
    Stanydale seer 107

Fit the Eighth: "As Ithers See Us" 109
    A town called toilets 111
    What's in a name? 112
    Dangerous liaisons 114
    Students 115
    Cruise ships 116
    Humours of Jarlshof 119

Fit the Ninth: Memorable Folk and Faux Pas 123
    Life's rich tapestry 123
    It's a small world 127
    Do mention the war 132
    Fine dining 135

Fit the Tenth: Hamefarin 138
    Redders of the lost kin 138
    Media moments. 143

Tailpiece 149

Excursuses
    Excursus 1. A Lady of Comfort and Kindness –
    Ellen (Nellie) Deans Allan 150
    Excursus 2. The Devil's Own – John Walker 164
    Excursus 3. Da Gulsa Shall and da Trowie Kapp 173
    Excursus 4. TripAdvisor Reviews 177

Glossary 183

PROLOGUE

It was the worst of smells; it was the best of smells. It was a fresh whiff of nostalgia that overcame me on a bright summer morning in 2005. A north-easterly breeze had wafted the olfactory quality of the Heogan Fish Meal Processing Plant (aka "da Gut Factory") across Bressay Sound to whet (or not) the pre-breakfast appetites of tourists arriving in Lerwick on the ferry from Aberdeen.

Rachel Carson, in her book *Silent Spring*, observed: *for the sense of smell, almost more than any other, has the power to recall memories...*

So true. The aroma that assailed my nostrils as I stood on the Lerwick dockside carried me back in time by thirty-six years to a morning when I was clocking-on for my very first proper job. That same Bressay breeze, with its omni-attendant malodour, had greeted me away back in 1969 as I awaited the foreman on the pier by Shetland Seafood's fish processing factory. Fishworker wasn't my choice as my first step into the world of full time paid work; the Lerwick 'Broo' office had made me an offer I couldn't refuse. My employment at the old HIB (Herring Industry Board) fish factory, owned by Shetland Seafoods, was to be my first taste of an officially recognised paid job, my first real pay-packet and my first contribution to the grasping hand of Roy Jenkins, Chancellor of the Exchequer.

Looking back to that summer of 1969 I remember it as an escape from the world of study, a time to make new friends, sharing new experiences and just working and living for the moment. If someone had predicted that many years hence I would be nasally absorbing the same aroma whilst waiting to collect my first clients for my new tour guiding business, I would have seriously doubted their sanity. However, in that summer of the first moon landings and the start of the violent 'Troubles' of Northern Ireland, the world was changing rapidly and plans I'd previously made to make my way in that world needed a review.

In Phase One of this book you can join me in that summer and in the 1950s and '60s Shetland I grew up in. I tell of my journey through my formative years and my search for a 'proper job'. During my growing-up decades Shetland was a very different place from the one we see today. Some would say that despite post-war austerity it was a much happier and more tolerant place in those pre-North Sea oil boom times. A time before the exponential growth of instant communication that fuel today's impatient expectations and desires.

Had I known then what I know now, would I have planned my future career carefully instead of reacting as I did to chance encounters? Perhaps it was the fickle hand of fate steering my course. A quote from a Burns poem comes to mind:

The best-laid schemes o' mice an' men,
Gang aft agley,

From this poem John Steinbeck took the title *Of Mice and Men* for his novel about displaced job seekers (more on Steinbeck in Phase Two). In Phase Two of this book I recall how through chance and accident I became a tour guide running my own business. I also tell of my experiences and people I met during eleven enjoyable years of guiding visitors through the length and breadth of Shetland.

(Author's note: *A few Shetland dialect words are scattered through the text and you may find the explanations of these in the Glossary helpful*).

Phase One

Fate leads the willing and drags along the reluctant.
(Seneca)

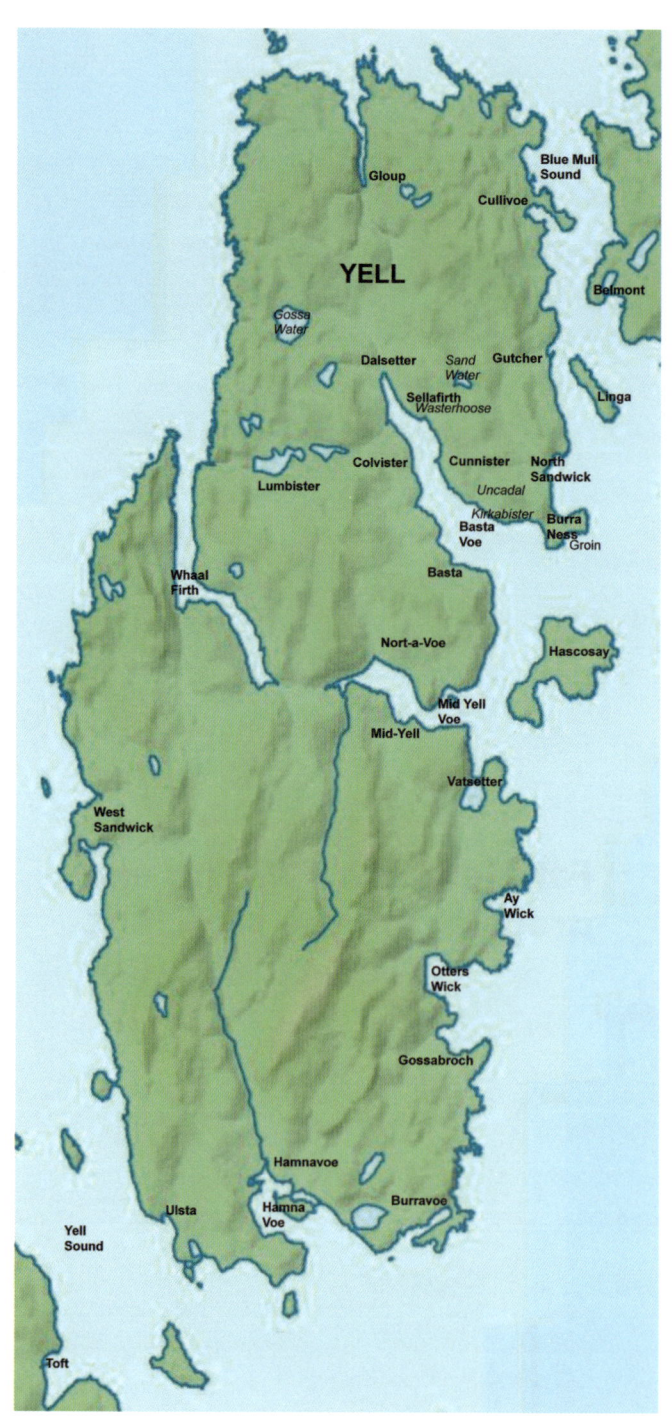

Map of Yell showing main settlements around Basta Voe.

Fit the First: Yell

If you really want to hear about it, the first thing you'll probably want to know is where I was born, and what my lousy childhood was like, and how my parents were occupied and all before they had me… So wrote J.D. Salinger to open *Catcher in the Rye* (incidentally another book title gleaned from a Burn's poem).

Fortunately for me my childhood was far from lousy and thankfully has few parallels with that of Holden Caulfield.

I was born in 1950 to crofting parents and grew up on their croft at Sellafirth, in the parish of North Yell, Shetland. Our rented croft, Wasterhoose, overlooked the long south-easterly fetch of Basta Voe, the North Sea's deep excursion into the island of Yell. Looking back, I feel that I was lucky enough to be born into a generation that saw the very last of the true crofting way of life or, as some might say, the 'real' Shetland. Little was I to know that my formative years in this fast disappearing lifestyle would equip me with insights that would become useful in my far distant career as a tour guide.

'Hame-aboot'

Wasterhoose was the most westerly of three croft houses, all built before 1851, and in close proximity, the other two being Midhoose and Aesterhoose. I, my parents, and my mother's parents lived in Wasterhoose. Wasterhoose was a two-up and two-down building with the barn and byre attached to the back with a byre extension across the east gable. Like so many 19th century, 'steen-biggit' croft houses it may have been raised to two storeys after the 1886 Crofting Act. Thus, two upstairs combed-ceiling bedrooms were above the downstairs 'but-end' and 'ben-end', a narrow, steep stairwell between gave access upstairs. A small front porch had been added giving access to both but and ben from the outside through internal doors. At some point the byre had been extended across the gable to incorporate part of Midhoose, which had once contained a shop when Sellafirth's onetime main public thoroughfare passed between it and Aesterhoose. In the mid-1960s my father and I demolished what was left of Midhouse to make a hard-standing outside the byre.

Wasterhoose and Aesterhoose with ruined part of Midhoose between; 1962.

    A mass-concrete, lean-to, single storey extension had been added to the rear wall of Wasterhoose; built long before the requirements of building warrants with reams of regulations bound up in yards of red tape. This, our 'back-hoose', served as kitchen and dairy. Cooking was on a peat-fired Enchantress stove with its permanent kettles on top for hot water, later replaced by a larger Wellstood, bought second-hand from the legendary Harry Hay's saleroom in Mounthooly Street, Lerwick. Occasionally the kitchen table was scrubbed down for the cutting up of 'home-kill'.
    A passageway ran from a door in the but-end between the back-house and the attached barn leading to the back-door exit into the yard outside. A side door in the passageway gave access to the barn. The barn was separated from the byre by a wooden partition with a door for access, another door led from the barn into directly into the yard. Outside, attached to the barn wall, was a weatherboard shed, partitioned inside to form a closet with its Elsan chemical toilet. Candles and matches to facilitate night-time visits had a permanent home on a 'rinner' just inside the closet door.
    Behind the barn stood the yard where the winter fodder was stored in the form of hay 'desses' and 'coarn skroos'. Set back from the yard was the stable for two horses, which in my time became a henhouse. There was a corrugated iron shed on the west gable of the Wasterhoose that stored various crofting implements and fishing gear as well as paraffin and petrol drums. Outside of the shed, peats were carefully built in large stacks to withstand the weather. Just west of the peat stacks was the midden for ash and animal dung in close proximity to the kale yard. Beyond that and surrounding the croft were various 'rigs' for coarn, hay, 'tawtees' and 'neeps'.

Aesterhoose, next door, was occupied by the Jamieson family until they moved away to Lerwick in 1960. Over time we were to purchase the crofts of Wasterhoose and Aesterhoose as well as Logie further up the hill to the east. Taken together the crofts then became, to all intents and purposes, a small farm.

All our water was carried in pails over one hundred yards uphill from the well, including the water for the 'kye' in the byre in winter. On a small wooden table in the corner of the passageway we kept two white enamelled pails containing drinking water. Our well was fed by a spring and kept clear of algae and insects by a brown trout captured from a burn and transferred to live happily in the well. It was not until 1962 that we got mains water piped into the house and byre from the Zetland County Council (ZCC) sponsored 'water scheme'. The back-hoose was then renovated and the old Wellstood stove was replaced with a more modern Truburn, bringing hot water on tap to kitchen sinks and a new indoor bathroom. A septic tank was dug and a toilet plumbed in. The water main connection brought to a thankful end the to-ing and fro-ing to the well and a not so fond farewell to the 'sae', the tin bath, and the Elsan closet, especially on bitter winter nights.

The introduction of mains water, and later mains electricity, was an attempt to halt the rapid depopulation of Yell by bringing living standards up to 20th century expectations. Back in the 1960s, excavating machinery was too heavy to dig water main trenches across the soft peaty moorland of Yell. This problem was solved by workmen using the traditional 'tushker' to cut a trench to accommodate the water pipes. Workmen were paid an extra sixpence a day for using their own 'tushker'. The trench was then backfilled with cut peat and the growing layer replaced on top making the trench across unspoiled moorland invisible. Such a contrast from today where lighter and more powerful excavators carve out black swathes across virgin moorland without any regard to the visual landscape. As a guide I was often asked by tourists: "Where do people get their water?" "Is your water safe to drink?" Which of course it is. Tactfully, I don't add that Shetland tap-water is probably more potable than water contained in the omni-present, supermarket-bought, travel-miled, money-wasting, litter-inducing, carbon-burning, sea-polluting, plastic bottles they are clutching.

For all of my childhood, and most of my teenage years, nights were lit firstly by wick and pressure paraffin lamps, then by bottled (Calor) gas lamps. There was no TV, so news, music and light entertainment came via a valve radio powered by lead-acid accumulator and dry batteries. Mains electricity arrived in Yell during 1968 after the long 'Yell for Light' campaign by islanders to get a power cable laid across Yell Sound from Mainland. I once asked my mother, if she could have just one, which of these utilities she would rather have… "Oh, da water every time!" Such was the difference unlimited piped water made to the winter drudgery of carrying water from the well in crofting life.

We had the traditional Shetland croft-house style, open 'paet' fire with its whitewashed 'shimley' in the but-end for a good few years until it was 'biggit-in' and a Rayburn stove installed. A rather battered, leather-covered, brass-studded, horsehair-filled sofa (actually a chaise longue) stood along the wall beside the window. I remember an almost ceremonial burning of this sofa and its replacement by a wooden 'restin-shair' that is still in my possession. The restin-shair came courtesy of my grandfather's brother who had it made, from a driftwood log he'd found during WW1, by well-known craftsman and joiner Andrew Williamson (Brake, Cullivoe).

The ben-end was where my grandparents slept and after their passing it became the best room for any relatives who came to stay. The standard and style of accommodation that I grew up in was little different from that found throughout Yell, or most of rural Shetland for that matter. When I came to guide visitors around the excellent Crofthouse Museum at South Voe, Boddam the smell of paet-reek from the open fire would take me right back to Wasterhoose in the 1950s.

Thinking back over the years it is difficult to pinpoint my earliest memory. It probably is sitting on my mother's lap looking up at the hissing Tilley pressure-lamp hanging beneath its large, round reflector-cum-heatshield, in the low but-end ceiling. I also remember my father carrying me outside to see the "day become dark", when we watched the kye and sheep lying down thinking it was night-fall. This would have been the total solar eclipse of 30th June, 1954.

Growing up with grand-folk

Today our standards of accommodation and speed of communication are far beyond anything my grandparents' generation could ever have imagined. My maternal grandfather, Peter Urquhart, was born in 1877 across the voe from Sellafirth in Basta. He eventually moved with his parents to live in Sellafirth, and all were in Wasterhoose by 1891. Like many crofter/fishing families of the time his parents had moved from croft to croft due to tenure changes, including being cleared (evicted) from Lumbister in 1867 by the infamous factor of the Garth Estate, John Walker.

My maternal grandmother, Ellen (Nellie) Deans Allan Nisbet, was born in 1881 at Cunnister at the other side of Basta Voe from Basta. Her parents had also endured the intimidation and eventual eviction from their croft at Uncadal (near Cunnister, North Yell) in 1868 by John Walker. She'd been given her name in honour of a most remarkable lady and philanthropist, Ellen Deans Allan (née Smith), wife of the Sellafirth Free Church Minister, the Rev. James Hamilton Allan; (*see Excursus 1*).

Even though the evictions of my great-grandparents occurred over eighty years before my birth, I would often hear the name "Walker" cropping up in conversation when I was a bairn and my grandfather calling him "da Deevil's own"; (*see Excursus 2*). Such was his influence on the people and crofting landscape that no man was ever hated so much throughout Shetland as John Walker. My link to this part of Shetland history later became a valuable asset in recounting the history of some derelict 'crofting toonships' to tourists.

I have just hazy memories of my grandmother Nellie, who died when I was four. With busy parents I spent a lot of time in my grandfather Peter's company, up until his death in 1959. He had gone to the 'haaf-fishing' as a boy then spent ten years on decked fishing boats. He left the fishing in 1906 for the Mercantile Marine where he served as an AB, and occasionally bosun, on various merchant vessels almost continuously for the next seven years. A year or so after marrying my grandmother he gave up 'sailing' due to progressive deafness. He then returned to the life of a crofter and took on work as a self-employed peat carter (earning him the nickname 'Paetie') and ploughman, using his horses. In today's parlance he had became an agricultural contractor, a designation that I'm sure would have amused him no end.

I was given both my Christian names (Peter and Allen) after my grandfather and grandmother. I was to be called Peter, but to avoid vocal consternation due to grandfather's deafness when calling my name, my middle name was used instead. Somehow the spelling of this got registered in the form of the English surname Allen instead of forename Allan, a mistake that often caused confusion when passed by phone or written down on documents, even to this day. My father blamed the registrar for misspelling, but I have my suspicions that he may have had a celebratory dram on the way to the registry office.

Grandfather Peter carting paets with white mare Keetie.

Like many of his generation grandfather Peter was a pipe smoker and a tobacco chewer, so I grew up with the smell of Walnut Plug and Black Twist. I used to help (most likely hinder) "Auld Daw", as I called him, with the crofting work. One incident that I still bear the scar of is when, aged about five, I fell onto the tip of a scythe blade and suffered a cut deep into the thenar of my left hand. Such a deep cut today would receive immediate attention from a doctor or hospital A&E, but in those days no quick transport or telephone was available, only Auld Daw's first aid. He pressed a freshly chewed tobacco plug onto the wound, telling me to "close de knave and birze on yon, an nivver du leet if hit swees". I don't remember if it 'sweed' and I guess I probably did 'leet' but the tobacco plug certainly did cauterise the wound.

I wish I could remember Auld Daw's stories that entertained me and the neighbour children. He taught me how to read before I started school which probably installed a lifelong love of books in me that introduced me to a wider world beyond the 'yerd-dek'. He also introduced me to a Shetland tradition that I found myself describing to visitors almost a lifetime later. This was the first of many shore fishing excursions to the 'craigs' that were near to Wasterhoose at a rocky outcrop called Brightnadek. Many a time I went shore fishing from that 'craig-steen' for 'sillicks' or 'pilticks'. This was done by a long bamboo pole known as a 'piltick waand' with a fixed line for casting a trace of home-made flies. However my first visit with Auld Daw to the craigs harked back to an earlier tradition where sillicks were attracted to the craig-steen by 'sprootin soe', then to be caught by a net known as a 'pock'. Auld Daw mashed up limpets in the 'soe-pot' then putting a handful of the mash into his mouth sprayed it out as form of projectile spitting over the sea by the craig-steen. Then it was my turn, a six year old following his grandfather's example. I 'sprootit soe', just once. Never, ever, again did I try that. Even now, sixty years later, recounting that episode brings back that ineffable flavour of 'lempit' soe to attack my taste buds.

Parents

Walter, my father, and Ann, my mother, moved to Yell from Burra in 1949 to look after her elderly parents and take on working the Wasterhoose croft. Crofting on the scale that they were to build up over the next thirty years in Sellafirth would have been almost unknown to my father, born and brought up in pre-war Burra.

Burra was a predominantly fishing community, so my father's first job on leaving school was 'yoag-dreggin' with his uncle Walter Jamieson to provide bait for fishing boats plying the 'haddock-line' fishing. Dreggin was done by a rowing boat which towed a specially made iron dredge over the bottom to dislodge and capture the large horse mussel (*Modiolus modiolus*). The flesh of these mussels was used to bait the hooks of long-lines set along the sea-bed to catch haddock. Elsewhere in Shetland large quantities of the smaller blue mussel (*Mytilus edulis*) were imported for use as haddock-line line bait. This method of line fishing for haddock no longer occurs in Shetland. Today mussel farming is a high value export industry; instead of importing tonnes of blue mussels Shetland now exports thousands of tonnes of them. Mussels are a "must-try" delicacy for visitors to Shetland and as a tour guide I would take great delight in telling how they would be eating what was once fishermen's bait.

In 1937, at age eighteen, my father left Burra and the fishing to follow the age-old Shetland tradition of a seaman in Merchant Navy. Two years later he found himself following another Shetland tradition by sailing for South Georgia for employment in the Antarctic whaling industry. He served the 1939-40 whaling

Father age 18. Photo from his seaman's I.D. card

season as the only non-Norwegian seaman aboard the whale catcher *Bouvet 3*, returning with her to Liverpool in May 1940. World War Two was now hotting up and in June 1940 he signed on BP tanker *British Lady*. After leaving the *British Lady* he served on a variety of merchant ships continuously throughout the war, fortunately without getting his feet wet. His last ship was the fleet oil tanker *Benton Field* which he joined in 1943 for her voyage to the naval base in Ceylon. He left this ship in 1945 with a broken leg from an accident on board. After a spell in hospital in Trincomalee (where he caught malaria) he returned home.

After a few months home at the summer fishing he shipped out for the Antarctic whaling once more. He spent an Antarctic winter of 1946 on the island of South Georgia and another summer whaling season before returning home in 1947. Many of our Yell neighbours were still taking part in the whaling industry up until it closed in 1964, so I grew up hearing stories of South Georgia, icebergs and the Antarctic. When many schoolboys of my generation in mainland Britain wanted to become train drivers, Shetland schoolboys (including me) had ambitions to become whalers. I was eventually able to visit the most fabulously spectacular island of South Georgia in 2016, but as a tourist, not a whaler.

Father (left) at Shackleton's Grave, Grytviken, South Georgia; 1947.

Like many Shetlanders of his generation, the money my father saved by overwintering in South Georgia was invested as a share in a small seine-net fishing boat, in my father's case the *Golden West*. The seine-net fishing method had gradually replaced long-line fishing as Shetland's fishing industry modernised and expanded. It could be said that monies earned at the Antarctic whaling pump-primed Shetland's post-war fishing effort, culminating in the modern fishing fleet and aquaculture industry we see today. Many tourists are fascinated to learn of Shetland's long whaling and fishing history. Today I can park near the site of a 19th-century whaling station opposite a modern mussel farm and relate a full circle of connections between whaling at both ends of the planet, fishing history and mussels.

In contrast Ann, my mother, had grown up on the Wasterhoose croft with her parents, sister and two brothers. She had done well at school, firstly at Gutcher then at Colvister, becoming top pupil for Shetland and Orkney.

A TOWN CALLED TOILETS   11

Mother (sitting) with her sister May and her brother John, Gutcher School; 1924.

Further education at the elitist Anderson Educational Institute in Lerwick was well beyond a crofting family's circumstances so precluded any chance of an academic career and she left school at fifteen. She once said that one of her saddest days was working in the neep-rig watching pupils walking along the road to school. As well as helping on the croft she took seasonal employment as a herring gutter, firstly at Cullivoe, and later at Lerwick. During the war years she worked in a munitions factory near Glasgow. Following the war it was back to work following the herring fishing from Lerwick in the summer south to Lowestoft and Great Yarmouth in the autumn and winter. "Da guttin", as the girls who followed the herring called it, was hard work, often for long hours when large catches of herring were landed. The herring girls stayed in specially constructed accommodation known as "da huts", where lifelong friendships were made and many 'funs' had. My mother always had a mischievous sense of humour. She would often recount her days in this industry, even in the latter months of her life in hospital she would relive the funs with the duty nurses during their tea-breaks.

Mother age 19.

A TOWN CALLED TOILETS 13

Mother at Cullivoe herring station; 1933. Back row: Bobby Smith, Yaafield, Bigton; Joey Jamieson, Aesterhoose, Sellafirth. Front row: Winnie Malcolmson, Sellafirth; Cecil Smith, Sandwick; Ann Urquhart, Wasterhoose, Sellafirth; George Sutherland (cooper), Bressay; Katie Malcolmson, Sellafirth.

Aunt May (left) and mother, Edinburgh; 1943.

Parents' wedding photo; 1948.

My mother could never, ever sit 'hawnd-idle', something that was ingrained to women of her generation from childhood. She was an expert knitter, especially in the Fair Isle pattern, and (although she would never have admitted it) probably as good as any in Shetland. Even at the age of ninety she was still able to knit Fair Isle gloves and berets for sale in local heritage centres. I recently re-discovered a Fair Isle all-over jersey she knitted for my eighteenth birthday that I had packed away and almost forgotten. Such was the quality of the work (and the expansion of my girth since then) that I donated it to Shetland Museum for their collection.

Mother knitting in Wasterhoose; 1967.

The croft by itself could never provide a living wage, so to supplement income my father worked by day as a roadman/labourer for Zetland County Council (ZCC). We always had a knitting machine in the house and, as the croft expanded, my father gave up his roadman work and became a home machine-knitter for a local company. He knitted the sections for garments and my mother grafted those together to produce the finished garment. Thus both my parents working from home was a flexible management of time, allowing crofting and knitting to work together. Economics and time management saw the kye being

18th birthday present.

sold off to be replaced by additional in-bye sheep, allowing more time to be spent on the knitting machine.

Time eventually came when the croft work was becoming too heavy for my parents to manage on their own, so they decided to retire. Retirement would have to be a clean break away from Wasterhoose and Sellafirth, otherwise they'd feel obliged to keep sheep on the croft with all the work that entailed. Where to retire to was the question. As far as my father was concerned Burra was the only option and, following the sale of the crofts, they moved to Meal in Hamnavoe in 1988. Sadly my father enjoyed only a brief retirement and died there after a short illness in 1995.

My mother lived on in Burra for another fourteen years until the ravages of old age and a lifetime of hard work made accommodation in a care home a more comfortable option for her to end her days. Sadly, like so many native Shetlanders who had given so much of their lives to Shetland during hard times and war, there were no places available in any of Shetland's excellent care homes. She, like so many others in her position, had to join a long queue for a place. Sadly she never saw the inside of a care home, eventually dying after a fall and a stroke during a prolonged stay in the Gilbert Bain Hospital waiting in the queue for a care home placement.

Fit the Second:
This Crofting Life

There were lovely things in the world, lovely that didn't endure, and the lovelier for that... Nothing endures. (Lewis Grassic Gibbon in *Sunset Song*.)

When I contemplate Shetland's crofting landscape it amazes me how quickly this has changed in my lifetime. My generation is the last in Shetland to have had practical experience of 'crofting life' and methods that had seen little change for centuries. I guess most tour guides today have no firsthand knowledge of how Shetland looked pre-1970s. The availability and development of farm machinery along with government subsidies gradually changed how crofters worked, but the biggest change to our crofting landscape is visual.

All change

Crofting in Shetland over the centuries was purely a subsistence occupation to feed the family; another occupation was needed for income. Tenancy of a subsistence croft often required a 'truck' arrangement with the landlord whereby all male members of the family were obliged to fish for him at the 'haaf'. The Crofting Act of 1886 gave security of tenure and the end of truck but the need for additional income continued. This could often mean long absences from home with employment in seasonal fishing, 'sailing' or whaling, leaving the womenfolk to do the croft work. By 1950 subsistence crofting in that sense had died out, but there was still the necessity for crofters to have a second income due to lack of good agricultural land. The difference between the Orkney and Shetland condition is often described thus: "An Orcadian is a farmer with a boat; a Shetlander is a fisherman with a croft". Due of course to the very different geology of the island groups that rewards Orkney with a relatively flat and fertile agricultural landscape.

In 1973 the UK joined the European Economic Community (EEC) and became part of its common agricultural policy. Almost overnight EEC subsidies raised the value of sheep to astronomical levels compared to what lamb and wool prices had been in the past. Very quickly Shetland's seasonally changing, multi-coloured field patchwork of hay, oats, barley, potatoes and kale vanished under grass to become uniform green swards of sheep pasture. Sheep numbers increased dramatically, probably three-fold in the twenty years up until 1990, reaching a staggering 400,000 head. Today, remaining fragments of the traditional crofting landscape are few and far between; thankfully I have been able to explain this to my visitors and pass on my experiences of how it used to be.

Visitors to Shetland see that we are fortunate to have fine museums as well as many excellent heritage centres covering all aspects of crofting life in times past. I don't consider myself particularly ancient, but I still get a sense of shock seeing crofting implements of my youth I hanging on walls instead of being used in the 'rigs'. Everyday objects I knew and used from inside our croft-house, barn or byre have become museum artefacts; names of these, like the objects themselves, have disappeared from everyday use. 'Kirns' and kirning for example; we made all our own butter and I can even remember a 'stave kirn' in use before the later handle driven one.

Growing the croft

The 1950s and 60s was a time when Sellafirth (and Yell generally) was becoming depopulated at an alarming rate. The Sellafirth shop closed in1959 as families left, so a shop came to us on Tuesdays and Fridays via the Scottish Co-operative Wholesale Society's (SCWS) grocery vans. The importance of these well-stocked mobile shops to the survival of rural communities, in which hardly anyone owned a car, cannot be overstated. Not only were these vans the only shop, their drivers carried local news, gossip and messages from village to village, croft to croft, person to person. The knowledge that a shop in the form of "Cop vans" would come to us twice a week must have helped my parents make the brave decision not to join the exodus, but to stay and make a living (at least in part) from the land.

My father must have taken to crofting like a 'selkie' to the sea. My earliest memories of crofting are that just about everything was done by hand, no mechanisation. Ploughing and carting was by horse. Hay and corn were cut with a scythe then raked or gathered by hand for curing and stacking. All croft work was subject to the vagaries of the weather which could easily set back days of labour.

Temptation to use a fine Sunday was resisted as this day was always kept as a day of rest. None of the family was staunch churchgoers, but tradition demanded that only essential daily work for animal welfare, such as feeding and milking, was done. Water from the well for use on Sunday was fetched last thing on Saturday evening. Auld Daw always had a thick moustache. When asked why, he said he needed it to take a drink of water in the dark. According to him the moustache would strain out any water 'klocks' that the drinking cup may have inadvertently picked up from the pail.

My first day on the croft; 1950.

With grandfather's dog, Pride.

Helping on the croft.

We had two horses. I can't really remember our white mare, Keetie, but I can remember Auld Daw ploughing with our other horse, Dodie, and with Keetie's replacement, the "black mare". I was often taken for rides on their backs and kept them both well supplied with sugar lumps, probably increasing Tate & Lyle's profits in the process. Sadly, progress dictated that first the mare then Dodie had to go and be replaced by a British Anzani Iron Horse. I missed Dodie for a while but very soon became enamoured with the new horse.

Grandfather Peter ploughing with Keetie at Uphouse, Sellafirth.

Father with cousins Joan, Peter and Bill Urquhart on the "Peerie Black Mare"; 1952.

The British Anzani Iron Horse was a marque of two-wheeled tractor that (along with BMB) had started the mechanical revolution of crofting in Shetland. Introduced in 1940, the Iron Horse had a 4-stroke, 6hp Anzani-JAP engine, giving a top speed of 4mph. It was a fairly sophisticated small tractor for its time; it had a centrifugal clutch, three forward gears and reverse. The wheel-track was adjustable from 24" to 36", and it came with a range of steel wheels, extension rims, pneumatic tyres or crawler track options, making it a machine that could cope with any terrain. It could be fitted with accessories such as ploughs, harrows, hoes and potato-lifters; it also could be hooked up to a trailer with a ride-on seat on the tow bar.

Although a small machine, the low gear ratio made it powerful for its size. I remember one time when a ZCC truck slid off the road into the ditch on the bend below Aesterhoose. The truck's crew fetched my father and the Iron Horse to tow it back on, which it did, but it took two men on each 'tram' to hold it down hard enough for the wheels to get enough traction on the road.

Our Iron Horse had two features which almost brought about its end (and nearly mine). Firstly, the tractor would remain stationary while in gear with the engine idling, only needing pressure on the throttle lever to start it moving. Secondly, the throttle lever was on the left-hand tram near the handgrip, just far enough from the ground for a five year old to reach. I don't remember exactly what my father intended to use the tractor for that day but I think he was showing off the "new horse" to my grandfather. When his back was turned to talk to my grandfather, the attraction of the shiny brass lever must have been too much. I reached up for it and pulled hard. The Iron Horse obeyed my command immediately and shot off down the slope with me standing watching its progress towards the 'banks-broo'. Fortunately my father was close enough at hand to sprint after it and stop it just before it made a ten-metre plunge into the 'ebb' below. I guess I got away with my 'misanter' because my father was too out of breath and my grandfather thought it hilarious and something that Dodie would never have done. I didn't try that stunt again.

Stock and land were improved over the years as my parents took on the adjacent crofts of Aesterhoose and Logie. At one time we had eight kye as well as Shetland sheep on the scattald and larger breeds of sheep 'inbye'. Even at its best the croft couldn't provide a living wage so my father worked for the ZCC as a roadman and was for a while employed in laying water pipes for the Yell water scheme. My mother kept an eye on the animals during the day, as well as knitting, and after a day's hard physical labour on the roads my father would turn to too and do the croft work in the evening. In time he gave up work for the ZCC and worked the croft along with fulfilling factory orders with the knitting machine. Without the Iron Horse we simply couldn't have worked our mixed arable and livestock crofts to the extent that we did. God knows how many hundreds of miles my father must have walked behind that tractor ploughing, harrowing and carting. Sometimes I used to think that it was a trial of strength between him and machine as to who would give in first. In the end I think they declared it a draw.

Father ploughing with the Iron Horse; 1964.

Crops were hay, ryegrass, 'coarn', 'tawtees', 'Shetland keel' and 'neeps'; all sown in the 'voar', tended during the 'simmer' and harvested by hand in the 'hairst'. Hay, ryegrass and coarn were cut by hand-scythe until mechanisation took over. The Mayfield Croft Tractor was another god-send that my father purchased a few years after the Iron Horse. Also two wheeled, it was much smaller than the Iron Horse and had a Villiers C25, 4-stroke engine, three forward and one reverse gear. This was fitted with a motor-scythe attachment that practically made the hand-scythe redundant overnight. I say almost redundant because we had a small area of meadow that was too boggy to cut with the motor scythe and was always mown by hand. The 'meedoo'-hay that came off this ground was much loved by the animals, and we used it as winter feed for the lambs we kept back as breeding stock. This area was known as "Halvers meedoo", which means shared-meadow. We shared the hay from this meadow with another two crofts, a practice perhaps going back hundreds of years.

The Shetland community tradition of doing a 'day's work' for your neighbours in return for them doing the same for you was still being practised when I was a bairn. Several men from other crofts would come and mow our hay and coarn with scythes and on other days my father would reciprocate on their crofts. These were exciting times for a small boy (no doubt getting in the way). The house would be busy with my mother cooking 'denner' for five or six men. These were generally young men who had returned from a season's whaling in the Antarctic and were full of yarns. More yarning would come in the evening when they would enjoy a bottle of beer at the end of a hard day's work.

Father with the Mayfield mower; 1985. Photo (c) Bill Urquhart.

Soon 'swaars' of the mown hay and ryegrass would be 'wharved' by raking then stacked on the 'hay-rigs' in 'coles' to dry further before being brought into the 'yerd'. In the yerd the hay would be built into a large 'dess', of which we had three some years. Building a hay dess took all day and was a combination of skill and art; it was a job that had to be done properly. The hay had to be packed evenly by trampling so that the dess had a symmetric cross-sectional shape preventing any chance of it being toppled by winter storms. It also had to have smooth sides so that there would be no water ingression causing hay to rot. Similarly, mown coarn was gathered into sheaves and 'stooked' to dry. Later the sheaves were built into 'skrövelings' on the rig for further curing before being 'hirded' to the yerd to be built into the winter 'skroos'. During winter months several days supply of hay and coarn were carried into the barn to be used daily to feed kye who spent their winter in the byre.

Tawtees were not just for our consumption but also cut up for animal feed during the winter, so we grew several varieties in fairly large rigs. In the voar, seed tawtees were set by hand along a ploughed 'fur' to be covered by the next passing of the plough. When these sprouted and grew into larger 'tawtee-shows' they had to 'haeped' using a hand hoe; thankfully this became a job that the Mayfield could do much more quickly with a hoe attachment. In the late hairst tawtees were lifted and 'hented' and some were carried into the barn to be stored in the 'tawtee-crö'. We also dug shallow pits in the tawtee-rig in order to store a larger quantity. Tawtees were poured into the pit and covered with earth to form a mound which was covered with insulating 'poans' to keep the contents frost free during the winter. Neeps were stored in the same manner

Building a hay dess. Left to right: Dogs Rollo and Jed; Willie Urquhart; Walter Fraser; Margaret Urquhart; Ann Fraser; 1967.

Father in the yerd with Jed.

after harvesting. I remember that we had a rig that the tractor couldn't plough and we 'delled' it using 'Shetland spades'. Tawtees were then planted in holes drilled using a 'dipplin-tree'.

Harvesting tawtees by delling and 'hentin' was back-breaking work, especially on a bitter day when the cold on bare fingers would be almost insufferable; the pain even getting under your fingernails. It was reckoned that if you held your hands in a bucket of cold water for as long as you could bear it, the cold wouldn't feel so bad when hentin; a remedy that I did try on occasion, but was totally unconvinced by this masochistic theory. A little known fact that I later picked up as a tour guide was that Beethoven employed a similar method before composing, to the point of being completely soaked!

We also grew the crofter's staple, 'Shetland keel'. Grown on every croft this was the only winter green vegetable available to both human and animal. Shetland keel has long thick stalk, broad leaves surrounding a very compact 'keel-heart' that often became an ingredient in mutton soup. Such was the importance of Shetland keel that it is celebrated in Shetland's most well-known dialect narrative poem – *Auld Maunsie's Crö* by Basil R. Anderson.

Wasterhoose and Aesterhoose with 'keel-yerd' and 'paet' stack; mid 1980s.

Today, yards flourishing with Shetland keel are a very rare sight and many a time on my tours I've been asked to do a 'keel-yerd' photo-stop when we encountered one. At Wasterhoose we set many hundreds of young 'keel-plants' every voar in our two keel-yerds. Although we grew some from our own seed in our own 'planticrub', most nursery 'keel-plants' we imported from Bressay, an island famous for hardy, good quality plants. Although still seen everywhere on the Shetland landscape, there are hardly any planticrubs in use today and are quite often labelled as 'brochs' on photos taken by less enlightened visitors.

'Paet' and 'haet'

Curing of 'paets', especially when we had open-hearth fires, seemed to take up the whole summer from 'flaying' and 'casting' the paets in May, to 'raising', 'turning' and 'rooging' the cut paets during the drying months of June and July. When dry these were 'hurled' then stacked by the roadside to await transport home. When we still had open fires at Wasterhoose we cut a huge quantity of paets, from something like three hundred yards or more of 'paet-banks'.

We had paet-banks in the hill behind the Logie croft and more at the head of Basta Voe. The latter were near the road just about a mile or so from home and were much easier to get to, and a lorry could be hired to bring them home. The Logie paet-banks could be cut deeper and gave a better quality paet but were not so accessible, even with a tractor and trailer. Eventually we gave up the Logie site and opened new paet-banks at Basta Voe. One of these banks had a thick layer of fine sand running through it at about one metre depth. This was always a nuisance as paets could easily break in two at the layer when casting and sand would blow into the eyes when dry paets were being handled. Many years later I was to discover that the sand layer was deposited by a localised tsunami that had swept in through Basta Voe and up over the land about 1500 years before.

After a wet summer, when drying had been poor, comments such as "all da haet wis in da wirkin o' dem" and "mair reek as haet" may have been passed. Traditional open-fires consumed vast quantities of paets and were only good for cooking one thing at a time in a pot or kettle suspended from above, or in a Dutch oven or on a 'braand-iron' over the glowing 'colls'. Those, like me, who remember how it used to be, will tell that sitting close to the fire in a draughty croft but-end ensured that your front was scorching and back freezing while most of the heat vanished up the 'shimley'. There was never any fuel poverty in a traditional Shetland croft house, just heat poverty.

Due to advances in stove design and better quality insulated houses, along with the comparative ease of oil or electric central heating, much less peat is cut in Shetland today. Stoves like the Victoress and Enchantress had built-in ovens and large hotplates and appeared in croft houses early in the 20th century. Not only did they make cooking easier and more versatile, but burned much less paets while heating rooms more evenly. The gradual introduction of these solid fuel stoves and later larger stoves such as Wellstood, Truburn and Rayburn with their hot water boilers dramatically reduced the quantity of paet cut.

The importance of paet, how it forms on our landscape, and the way we used it is still of great interest to the tourist while the active paet-bank is a must-have photo opportunity. As with the harvesting of hay and coarn, giving a 'day's work' tradition also applied to the cutting and curing of paets. Men came together to do the 'casting' for each croft in turn and later in the summer the women would periodically meet in the 'paet-hill' to share the 'raising', 'turning' and 'rooging'.

Sharing the workload in this way was as much a social occasion for the community as it was a necessity in remote areas. Those in the community who were unable to work their own paets, through old age or infirmity, would have it done for them and would offer payment for the work, often just a token payment would be accepted. Today, I guess some highly paid city consultants would describe this as "social bonding", but in past times survival depended on your neighbours' co-operation. You didn't have to like your neighbour but you sure as hell needed to get on with them. In recent times this maxim has been lost in some parts of Shetland where attempts to repopulate failed and continue to fail. Sadly, these failures are mainly due to incomers bringing the urban social intolerances they were trying to escape from with them.

A cordial visit

One summer when I was about sixteen I'd been casting paets for an elderly widow lady who lived on her own. My arrangement with her was that I'd cast her paets in my own time in the early summer and let her know when I'd finished. The weather hadn't been good so I felt under a bit of pressure to get the job done. One fine Friday morning I decided that I'd finish the job in a day if I made an early start. Her paet-bank was over a mile from Wasterhoose and since I hadn't bothered to take any food with me I stopped the passing Co-op grocery van in the late morning to buy a snack. As usual I exchanged friendly banter with Basil the driver and bought a packet of Jammy Dodger biscuits (on his recommendation) and a bottle of orange squash. There was a notice in the van advertising a dance in the North-a-Voe hall that evening that I fancied going to. I resolved not to waste an hour or so returning home at 'denner' time; Jammy Dodgers would sustain me until I'd finished and I'd have time to get cleaned up, have my tea and cycle to the dance in the evening.

On the way home for my tea before setting out for the dance I called along the lady to let her know that her paets were done. As was the custom she insisted on paying me and I responded by taking just a nominal sum. Then she asked, "Wid du tak a gless o' cordial?"

I was in a hurry, but it would be rude to refuse and I was thirsty, so I agreed. From the deep inner recesses of a press she brought out a dark and dusty glass bottle with no label and poured me out a large tumbler full of reddish cordial. I thanked her and arranged to 'hurl' her paets and stack them by the road later in the summer. Being in a hurry I drunk the cordial in two long swallows, said my goodbyes and set off for home on the bicycle. Before I'd cycled the half mile to our gate for the track leading into Wasterhoose I was having difficulty steering a straight line and keeping my balance. I dismounted at the gate with a spinning head and didn't try to remount again. I think the bike supported me as I walked in the track to the house.

My father watched my progress, then said, "Whit's du been up tae?"

"Ah'm been feenishing yon wife's casting an steppit alang her hoose ta tell her."

"Did shu mak de ony denner?"

"No," says I, "shu poored me aff a muckle tumbler o' cordial."

"Boy," he says, "yon wisna cordial, yon's her ain rhubarb wine at du's been at."

The effects of sinking almost a pint of potent rhubarb wine straight into an empty stomach soon wore off after I had my tea. I did cycle to the dance but kept well clear of alcohol that night.

A 'caa' and 'clootie-dugs'

Many generations of breeding has 'hefted' native Shetland sheep to the unfenced communal grazing pastures of our hills, thus co-operation with neighbour crofters is essential when it comes to sheep management. Before the days of the EEC membership most of the sheep we owned grazed along with other crofters' hill-sheep on the Sellafirth 'scattald'. Sheep had to be gathered three times a year and driven down from the scattald and this was very much a communal effort. A day to 'caa' the hill would be set by mutual agreement, with each crofter having an area of hill to 'gather' using collie-dogs. Sheep, driven from each gathered area, would merge at the 'crö' where they were to be 'punded'. Droves of gathered sheep converging under the control of crofters' dogs would behave reasonably well until faced with the prospect of entering the crö, and this is where the fun would begin.

Just about all the women in the community would gather on both sides of the drive leading to the crö to encourage passage of sheep through the entrance. Often the lead group of sheep would balk at the entrance and try a sidewise dash to freedom through the onlookers. The traditional response to this was for women to shake and flap 'haps' or 'peenies' (colloquially known as 'clootie-dugs') at the sheep in an attempt to turn them back. More often than not, instead of having the desired effect of redirecting the wayward to the entrance, some would turn back into the oncoming flock in defiance of dogs and crofter-drovers. This would trigger more breakaways, more waving of clootie-dugs and so on. A sort of semi-controlled chaos would then ensue as an assortment of clootie-dugs flapped even more vigorously: over excited collies ignored whistles and shouted commands; exasperations and tempers of drovers would rise exponentially; a variety of descriptive language aimed at dogs and sheep became more colourful and unprintable. Eventually breakaways were thwarted, escapees 'punded', dogs, sheep and crofters quieted as clootie-dugs returned to their wearers' shoulders and waists.

The Sellafirth crö was situated close to the Church of Scotland manse. A minister who stayed there in the early 1960s often came into the manse garden to observe the entire goings on. One caa had been a bit more fraught than usual, thus causing the minister to observe to a passer-by that dogs worked much better when swear words accompanied the commands!

Collies and 'kollies'

A croft couldn't operate without working collies. We always had two dogs, an older one and a younger one, so that when the older dog passed on we had one fully working while a new dog was training. All our dogs enjoyed living in the house with us, no cold nights in outside sheds for them. My father's reasoning was that we couldn't make a living without the dogs, therefore they were entitled to the same creature comforts as us. Growing up with dogs I guess I became their best friend when they weren't working. All had the usual doggie names: Lark and Pride (my grandfather's dogs); then, Tip, Glen, Meg, Jed, Rollo and lastly, Mirk. None, except 'trial-bred' Glen, had formal pedigrees. Each had a different personality and eccentricities but all were good working dogs apart from Meg, who had absolutely no interest in sheep.

*Neighbours at the Sellafirth crö after the caa.
Left to right: John Williamson, Isa Williamson, Jessie Henry,
Laurie Williamson, Alex Henry, Drew Williamson, Katie Williamson; 1950s.*

*Rooing and clipping. Sheep, Left to right: Ann Fraser
Allen Fraser (the author), Walter Fraser; 1967.*

I was only a toddler when Lark was around so I just have faint memories of him. However, he seems to have been the most eccentric of all our dogs. When I arrived on the scene he appointed himself as my protector so only members of the household were allowed to pick me up; if a visitor looked to pick me up he would place himself between me and them with fangs bared. Lark had boundless energy and stamina, so much so that a hard day's caa of hill sheep wasn't enough fun for him; as soon as the crö 'grind' closed he would immediately pick a fight with the nearest dog! He would regularly set off on his own to patrol the croft boundaries to ensure no rabbits would get near crops; any rabbit that strayed too far from a burrow soon became an ex-rabbit. One winter's day my grandfather had blacked out and collapsed in a field out of sight of the house. Fortunately, Lark was with him and ran to the house to raise the alarm. Thanks to Lark help arrived in time and grandfather Peter made a full recovery.

With grandfather's dog Lark.

Glen was good at sheep but loved working kye, and we could rely on him to go on his own to fetch the kye home from the distant croft of Logie. Once, a passing motorist on holiday from a large cattle farm in Scotland observed him doing this and offered a large sum to buy him then and there. My father refused his offer. When I was judged to be old enough, I was allowed to use the dogs to round up the winter 'aalie'-lambs we were keeping for the next year's breeding stock. The idea was that the dogs would probably train me how to work sheep. Aalie-lambs were kept inside at night (or during snowy weather) in the 'lamhoose' where they were fed hay from racks or a mixture of chopped up tawtees and oats in troughs.

Some feeding of the aalie-lambs, and kye in the byre, was done in the evening which, being winter, was dark. In my grandfather's time, for lighting he used a homemade 'kollie' lamp which he kept in the 'aeshins' just beside the door. This was an empty 1lb tin of Lyle's Black Treacle with a hole punched in the lid to accommodate a metal pipe that carried a lamp wick. The tin was filled with paraffin and the wick, when lit, gave an adequate light. I even made a replacement for this that we used until my father obtained a ship's lantern that gave a better light and was infinitely safer. I used to think that the Lyle's tin kollie was unique to us, that is until I saw an identical arrangement in a traditional house museum on the world's most remote inhabited island, Tristan da Cunha.

'Twallin' kye and six score draws

Before we expanded the crofts and built up more stock we had just two or three kye of the native Shetland breed. These were kept in the byre stalls all winter and let out in the spring when grass became available. At that time most of our crop-growing rigs were unfenced so, in the summertime, kye had to be tethered by a long rope staked to the ground, allowing them to graze in a large circle. This arrangement required that each animal had to be 'flit' to a new patch of grazing several times a day. The kye we used for milk had to be milked as well as flit about midday. Sometimes this job of 'twallin da coo' fell to me when I was deemed to be strong enough to pull up and drive the tethering stake into the ground. The job of making the wooden stakes and 'swills' for the animal tethers eventually became one of my chores. Driftwood was used for this purpose, and once shaped, holes for the rope were bored in the wood by use of a red hot poker. Another skill set that I was taught by my father in relation to this was how to splice rope and tie a range of knots.

The Sellafirth shop had closed by 1959 as island depopulation quickened, and by the early 1960s we were the only croft in the townships of Sellafirth and Cunnister that still had kye. By now we had a mix of Shetland kye and Angus-Shorthorn cross with suckling calves. As we were now supplying milk to most of the remaining families in these townships we really needed a dedicated milking cow, but one such as a Friesian or Holstein was well beyond our budget. My father had entered a football pool coupon for many years but had never won more than a few shillings. Just at the time that we needed a milking cow his coupon came up with a correct forecast of six score draws plus two no score. Often this would have meant a very large payout but on this occasion the payout was relatively low, however he still received the respectable sum of £36 (about £700 today). My father had long coveted a Friesian and this windfall allowed the purchase of a young Friesian milker just at the time we needed one.

In buying this cow my father had forgotten one salient fact about Friesian kye; they are extremely long-legged compared to the kye we already owned.

Father with Shetland cow 'Norma'; 1967.

When the cow was delivered my father led it proudly towards the open byre door, where both he and the cow came to an abrupt halt. There was just no way that cow would ever pass through the byre door unless on bended knees, and that would never happen; my father now knew that and more importantly so did the cow. Fortunately the weather was benign and his pride and joy was tethered outside for the next day or so while we heightened and widened the access to the byre.

Onybody spoken fur de 'faa'?

Home-killed mutton formed a substantial part of our crofting diet and, having no electricity, had to be preserved in salt brine over the winter. Brine was made up from granular salt and water from the well. A potato was used as a makeshift hydrometer to judge the specific gravity of the brine; salt was dissolved until the potato just floated to the surface. A proportion of mutton was removed from the brine and 'reestit' by the paet fire. Once a crofter's winter staple diet, it amuses me to see reestit mutton now promoted all year round as a "you must try" Shetland delicacy. Home-kill sheep were our own stock from the scattald – 'cast yowes' were mostly for the 'saat-tub', while one to two-year-old hogs were killed and hung for use as fresh meat; a job that I often helped my father with. By my early teens I had learned to 'buggi-flay' and butcher the carcass correctly, skills which I haven't used in a very long time. With the arrival of mains electricity the saat-tub was replaced by a large-capacity chest-freezer and fresh mutton became available all year round.

Nothing was wasted. The skins (with the wool on) were salted to store for later curing into sheepskin rugs; we carried the 'faa' to the shore to be cleaned and washed in seawater. This was so the stomachs could be used as bags to be stuffed and boiled as puddings. Dialect words associated with home-kill are now becoming a thing of the past; not many today can recite the dialect names of a sheep's faa – 'da King's hood', 'da lackie', 'da lungie' and 'da spaarl'. As was often the case, several sheep would be home-killed at the one time and some meat would be offered to neighbours without any sheep of their own. Also, there would be more faa available than the owner could use, and these would be cleaned and given away too.

Sometimes a neighbour, aware of a home-kill in the offing, would ask for the faa. It is now illegal to comply with this request. Home-kill is still legal in crofting areas, but because of crazy EU regulations it is illegal to give away any part of the sheep, or even for a visitor to eat any of it at your table. Today when visitors (often from cruise ships) request "Gee, say something in your wonderful language," the reply is sometimes "Hase onybody spoken fur de faa?"

Fit the Third: Pastimes and Past Times

For will anyone dare to tell me that business is more entertaining than fooling among boats? He must have never seen a boat, or never seen an office, who says so. (Robert Louis Stevenson.)

The interdependence of croft and boat was such that all crofts needed access to the sea and foreshore. For centuries the use of a boat was a necessity and, in more modern times, for recreation. Before Shetland's road building programme began in about 1848, practically all transport was by sea; crofters used small boats with the same familiarity as we use cars today. Generations of boat handling skills made Shetlanders ideal boat crews for the Arctic whaling trade and a prime target for the Press Gangs of the Royal Navy during the Napoleonic Wars.

The 20th century saw sailing regattas of so called Shetland Model boats becoming popular in communities all across Shetland. In the mid to early 20th century larger settlements throughout Shetland had their summer regatta days, where boats from neighbouring communities would arrive to race against local boats. In the early days crofters working foweraereens with the traditional dipping lug square-sail would race against each other. As time progressed these would be fitted with fore and aft rigs and boats were being built purely for regatta sailing. During the second half of the 20th century the design of specially built regatta boats continued to evolve so that they no longer resemble the traditional foweraereen. Now an ugly hybrid between a traditional boat and a conventional sailing dinghy, the cost of building and rigging such boats is well away from anything that the crofter could have imagined. Sadly, regatta days are now no longer the all encompassing community social events they once were.

Staples

Fishing from a small boat in the voes and sounds between the islands provided a diet of fresh fish, some of which would be salted, air dried and kept for the winter. Dried, salt fish such as piltick, whiting, ling or cod, was an essential part of the crofter's winter larder, along with salted mutton, potatoes and butter. Dried fish is rehydrated by soaking in water overnight then boiled with potatoes and eaten with butter. For many in hard times dried fish and potatoes were just about the only food they had. Known as the 'eela', this kind of fishing from a traditional 'foweraereen' (or its modern, 40hp-driven fibreglass replacement) is still a pastime enjoyed today. Salted and dried fish is no longer a necessity but many regard it as a delicacy; visitors to Shetland can still see strings of whiting, ling and piltick drying outside modern homes.

A haven of nostalgia, the Crofthouse Museum, South Voe, Boddam. Peat fire, stave kirn in the foreground, salt fish and reestit mutton hanging up.

For most traditional crofts access to the foreshore and the 'ebb' was required to harvest 'waar' driven ashore by winter gales to manure rigs. Here, too, sheep could graze on 'tang' and waar to supplement their diet. In times of hardship the ebb could provide income by hentin 'wylks' for sale to supplement income. Such was the importance of the foreshore to the crofter that banning access to it was one of the extreme methods used by John Walker (infamous factor of the Garth estate) to evict his crofter tenants.

Eela

I guess you can take the man out of the croft, but you can't take the boy out of the boat. We always had a boat, in fact two at first. Grandfather Peter had a 'sixaereen' called the *Annie* that he owned with his two brothers. I don't remember it being afloat, but do remember often being lifted aboard it in its winter 'noost' when I was very small. It came to a sad end in a southeast gale when a storm surge swept into the noost and broke it up. Eventually the broken sides were salvaged and were made into a 'snaa-böl' for sheep to shelter at in winter. The other boat we kept pulled up in our 'noost' at Bayanne, just below the croft. This was a foweraereen built of larch on oak with a keel length of about nine feet. I don't remember the first time I was taken to the eela, but ever since then I was looking to 'geng aff' any time that I could persuade my father to take me, not that he took much persuading.

Father at the eela in Basta Voe. Photo (c) Bill Urquhart.

The eela was mostly a summer pursuit, usually in the evening when the long hours of daylight are just punctuated by a few hours of 'simmer-dim'. There is nothing to better the quiet pleasure of an 'andoo' along the shore on a calm evening after sunset with shadowed hills reflected in still waters. Evenings when the quality of silence in the 'hömin' is punctuated only by 'antrin' drumming of a distant 'horse-gook' and the gentle splash of the oars. Sometimes oar blades leaving the water lift and drip trails of fiery 'mareel' onto the darkening waters. You'd be hard pushed to find anywhere in the world that can compare with the tranquil beauty of a Shetland voe on a summer night.

I remember one late summer evening at the eela when I was quite young; my father had taken me out in the boat along with my grandfather and my aunt's husband from England. It was nearly dark as we returned to the shore and we could see the light from Wasterhoose but-end window. My grandfather remarked on how bright the light was to my mother who had come down to meet us at the noost. My mother replied that she'd left my aunt (her sister May) to fill up and light the Tilley pressure lamp. My father immediately sussed out something was wrong and headed for the house as fast as he could. He told us later that when he came into the but-end where my aunt was sitting he'd been almost blinded by the brightness of the lamp. He'd said nothing but carried the lamp outside and, well away from the house, very slowly released the pressure to put it out. My aunt had refilled the lamp in the shed and, in the semi-darkness, had mistaken a petrol flask for the one containing paraffin for the lamp. My father had defused a potentially devastating petrol bomb!

We had no outboard motor, so most of our fishing was done by rowing within the confines of Basta Voe, which is a fairly large stretch of water. Here we would fish mackerel and pilticks in the summer by handlining a 'dorro' with its weighted trace of flies. My father would andoo while I fished; once I was judged old enough to pull the oars then we would occasionally swop over. In time I was allowed to take the boat out onto the voe myself. The yardstick for this was that if I could pull the boat down the beach and launch it myself then I would be strong enough to row it anywhere in the voe. One evening, when in my early teens, I had gone out by myself and had rowed well out to the mouth of the voe. Just as I was starting to row back a bank of fog rolled in off the open sea so that I quickly lost sight of the surrounding landmarks and shorelines. Very soon it became a 'steekit-stumnaa' and visibility had dropped to just a few yards in a dank, grey circle around the boat. This didn't worry me overmuch heading into a familiar landlocked voe; if I kept rowing with the light breeze astern I would find the shore easily enough.

Unfortunately the breeze dropped to a complete calm and, having no compass, I was completely 'wilt'. I rowed on slowly for about ten minutes or so, but in a steekit-stumnaa time and distance cease to seem normal, and there was no guarantee that I hadn't rowed a circle and was heading back out to sea. I stopped for a while in my silent, grey circle to listen for any helpful land sounds; silence was broken only by the occasional whooshing of a distant 'neesick' surfacing. Sound carries well over water, so it occurred to me that if I whistled the dogs at the croft would hear me and run to the noost to greet me. Not finding me there, and if I whistled again, they would start barking. This I did a few times and soon heard their chorus of barks and I could row in the direction of the sound. Soon I could 'scrime' a familiar shoreline. In fact, I had been on a reasonably good course and was closer to the noost than I thought.

Basta Voe today looking southeast towards the entrance.

Several times a year my father and I would row all the way out of Basta Voe into the open Colgrave Sound and around Burra Ness headlands. Here we would fish for large pilticks near a 'baa' called Da Groin where lay the sunken wreck of the trawler *Jackdaw*. A few good catches of these would ensure that we had enough fish to salt in brine then air dry to last us the winter. The round trip to Da Groin involved rowing a total distance of at least eight miles.

Of course there are always superstitions involved with boats and fishing; a strict protocol has to be observed when onboard. A boat always has to be turned 'sungaets', to turn a boat 'widdergaets' against the sun is regarded as a cardinal sin. There are lots of taboo words never to be used at sea, but substitute names can be used instead, such as 'dratsi' for otter and 'upstander' for a minister of the church. I remember once my father and I had a long, hard row out to Da Groin against the wind and tide; "a sair peck" he called it. When we got there the fish were just not cooperating. Each time we would row across our 'meid' we either caught nothing or just a single fish. It looked like we were going to have a poor return for our hard row. It was my turn on the dorro and I 'hailed' just one small piltick. My father said, "Spit in his mooth an slip him back."

I'd never heard of this before, said nothing, but did as I was bid and spat in the fish mouth and returned it alive. Next time we crossed the meid I started catching good-sized fish and each time we caught more; eventually we came home with one of the best catches we ever had from there.

Even after the arrival of electricity and the freezer, dried salt fish remained part of our diet, not a necessity, but just because we liked it. Not everyone shares the average Shetlander's taste for salt fish. When I was quite young I had fractured an arm and had to keep it in a sling for a bit. This was back in the days of the government's Welfare Foods programme to make the British Nation healthy by force-feeding children cod liver and concentrated orange juice. Our GP called along one day to see how I was doing, just as my mother was boiling salt pilticks for dinner and, of course, he was offered to partake. He declined, exclaiming, "Salt fish looks like firewood, tastes like firewood, and has exactly the same nutritional value as firewood!"

Ebb

As a youngster I found the 'ebb' a source of endless ploys as well a place for soaking up natural history, not least by an occasional unscheduled dip the sea. It was a place where we youngsters could fish for crabs or sillicks from the rocks, sail home-made model boats made from 'seggies', or barrel staves, or even deluxe versions fashioned from National Dried Milk tins. The inner part of Basta Voe is relatively shallow with a sandy bottom so dries out for a long way with low water at spring tides. On such occasions we would venture out onto the sand with spades and buckets to capture 'spoots' and 'smisslens' to take home for the pot. Once a supplement to the crofter's diet, spoots are now often seen as expensive starters in high-end restaurants or on TV programmes such as *Masterchef*.

Sellafirth today looking towards the shallow head of Basta Voe. Wasterhoose and Aesterhoose centre left; Bayanne by the shore; Hall far right with red roof. Photo © Rory Gillies Shetland Flyer Media.

The ebb was where 'wrack-wid' came ashore when wind and tide was favourable. This in the days before container ships when it wasn't uncommon for whole or partial deck cargoes of timber to be washed overboard. Flotsam and jetsam carried into Colgrave Sound and Hascosay Sound by tidal currents would get blown into Basta Voe by southeasterly gales. From an early age

I was very much into an age-old Shetland pastime (an obsession for some) of beachcombing. In favourable conditions (often into the teeth of a southeasterly gale) it was not uncommon to set off at first light to walk along several miles of shoreline in search of washed up driftwood. In an island with no trees, timber was an expensive commodity to import, so wrack-wid was much welcomed and found a variety of uses around the croft. Once rescued from the ebb, the spoils of the sea would be laid up well above the beach and high water mark. Once wood was laid up it was taboo for anyone but the finder to remove it. Depending on size it would be carried home or collected by boat in fine weather.

One afternoon, sometime in the early 1960s when my father was away at work, I came home from school to find the house empty. There was no sign of my mother or our two dogs anywhere around the croft or in the outhouses. Worried, and not sure what to do next, I whistled to see if the dogs were in earshot. Soon they both appeared from the direction of the shore below the croft. I hurried down there and looked over the banks-broo to find midder busy laying up long planks of good quality timber onto an already large pile. As I looked out across the water more and more of the same were drifting towards the shore. I joined in to help my mother and by the time my father came home we'd salvaged the lot. A few days before the deck cargo of timber had shifted onboard a ship as it was passing the east of Shetland and bundles of timber had been jettisoned. Providence, in the form of wind and tide, had driven most of the timber from a bundle ashore below the croft, enough for us to re-roof the byre.

One fruitful morning I laid up twenty railway sleepers from the ebb. Another time I collected several sealed, grey-painted metal containers with US Navy Emergency Rations stencilled on them from the 'shoormal'. These I carried home and opened with a can-opener. Inside each I found: a tin of water (didn't drink it); biscuits (hard); pemmican (nice); chocolate tablets (just ok); milk tablets (disgusting).

As well as deck cargo, other useful articles got washed overboard, especially in the Cold War days when the Soviet fishing fleets plied their trade in Shetland waters. Manila ropes, nets, corks, wooden barrels and wooden fish-boxes all found a useful home in crofts all across Shetland. Russian trawler crews were happy to trade such items for (to them) luxury goods such as our mass-produced ball point pens. Shopping catalogues were also popular, presumably to take home to show their families how we lived in the decadent west. Russian fishermen also seemed to have unlimited supplies of cigarettes to trade; unfortunately these were of the hardly palatable "blow-pipe" variety that had the tobacco at the end of a cardboard tube.

Basta Voe was a favourite anchorage for Russian trawlers seeking shelter from storms or for effecting repairs. One evening John (a Lerwick lad on holiday in Sellafirth) and I rowed out to a trawler with a selection of items to trade and were made welcome by the captain and crew. Only the mate had enough English to hold a conversation and he gave us a guided tour of the trawler. Next we were invited to meet the captain in his cabin for a dram; a shot of vodka drunk straight down followed by the traditional zakuski (a salt pickle snack). By his desk was a picture of a man and he asked (via the mate) if we knew who it was. They both laughed at our uncertainty of choosing between Stalin and Lenin; it was Lenin. We then were invited to have our evening meal with the crew, which we did. The meal was fish accompanied by potatoes, black bread and fig tea, none of which was terribly appetising to our palates. They were genuinely pleased to have us aboard to talk to (through the mate) but were guarded in answering our questions on the Soviet Union, perhaps due to a "Party man" being on board.

Today, thanks to the invention of the standardised shipping container and purpose-built container ships, wrack-wid and other bounty is a thing of the past. In the 1950s and early '60s if I found a plastic bottle in the ebb it was such a rarity I took it home. Today much of the ebb all along the high water mark is a disgusting tangle of washed-up, broken plastic shards, plastic string, plastic bags, off-cut polypropylene fishing net and rope, plastic bottles, broken plastic containers, broken plastic floats and plastic fish boxes. In some areas this unholy tangle is added to by discarded material from the aquaculture industry. The source of most sea-driven plastic waste is not Shetland, but the rivers of Europe, Britain and the Americas that discharge the products of our takeaway and throwaway society into the North Sea and the Atlantic. Added to this are the carelessly dumped off-cut nets and ropes from the fishing fleets of Continental and American nations. Every spring, all across Shetland, volunteers remove tons of plastic and other rubbish the sea brings each winter to our most popular beaches. This organised community effort is called the Voar 'Redd' Up, but unfortunately, with the best will in the world, there are many remote coves and beaches that cannot be reached and the indestructible plastic detritus continues to accumulate.

'Trootin'

The 'ebb' was also where I set my first 'troot' net. Grandfather Peter and my father had acquired an old herring net and cut it down to a smaller size so that I could stretch it down in the ebb at low tide. The bottom of the net was weighted down by 'link-steens' and had corks attached to the balk-rope along the top. When the tide came in the net would rise like a curtain in the water to snare any unsuspecting sea trout that came along. When the tide went out any fish caught were left high and dry in the ebb to be collected. The trick was to get there as soon as the tide was low enough to retrieve the fish, otherwise a gull or an otter would beat me to it.

Basta Voe was a great voe for sea trout and grilse salmon. My father and I would often set off with waders and twelve-foot greenheart rods; it was not uncommon for us to come home with several good-sized sea trout, having returned several smaller ones. In time the greenheart rod and the centre-pin reel gave way to the handier fibreglass spinning rod and reel. Sadly, sea trout and grilse are a rare sight in Shetland voes today due to a number of factors; not least to the expansion of the salmon farming industry creating hot-spots of sea-lice.

Several burns discharge into the ebb around Basta Voe and they became part of nature's playground for me. These burns also let sea trout up to their headwater lochs and into the spawning burns that feed the lochs. Lochs also became a favourite haunt of mine after autumn rains had allowed the passage of fresh-run sea trout. Not having a fly rod in those days I would spin for the sea trout in the voes and lochs; if this method saw little success I had a plan B. This cunning plan came in a traditional practice of fishing, probably now illegal in Shetland, but legal in Norway, called otter boarding. Someone (at woodwork class at school if I remember correctly) had shown me how to make a small otter board that was hinged and could fold in half to be carried in my fishing bag.

An otter board is a short plank of wood with one weighted edge so that it floats vertically in the water with about eighty per cent submerged. When attached to a light hand-line it can be controlled by walking along the shore to sweep out into the loch fishing flies on droppers attached to the hand-line. This method can be fairly deadly to fish and allows a much larger area of the loch to be covered than by conventional angling. The otter board is of course hated and condemned by purist anglers catching fish for sport. I, on the other hand, found this just as enjoyable as any other method. To me otter-boarding, like using the troot-net, was part of my heritage to fish for the pot, and as such I never took more fish that we could use.

Regatta days

In the days before mussel farms, Basta Voe was the best voe for regatta sailing in Shetland. Its long aspect, combined with the semi-circular Sella Firth, made for excellent sailing and afforded unrestricted views of the regatta course. Basta Voe Regatta as I first remember it, in common with other island regattas, was very much a local holiday and big social occasion. As well as the sailing races there would be land sports, motorcycle trials and in the evening a prize-giving followed by a variety concert and dance in the village hall.

The Sellafirth pier with its 'steamer's store' was where the starting/finishing gun for sailing races was fired, and the focal point for pier-head experts and other local worthies to gather. Just above the pier was the shop, where soft drinks could be purchased for those too young to take part in the sailing. I remember one particularly rainy regatta day sheltering in the steamer's store with my bottle of Hay's lemonade listening enthralled to Yell's legendary storyteller, Bruce Henderson (aka Brucie a' Arisdale). Today, thanks to the foresight of the School of Scottish Studies to make oral recordings in the 1950s and 1960s, we can listen to tales from Brucie and other Shetland storytellers such as Tom Tulloch by virtue of the internet (on the *Tobar an Dualchais* website).

Shetland Model boats, I remember from days before modern, ugly hybridisation, had captivating sounding names to small boys and sailors alike. Basta Voe had the *Freya*, *Bar-Ann*, *Minaroo* and *Miss Gadabout* while my great-uncle's boat had the unflattering name of the *Orange-Box*! Visiting boats from

Unst included *Mareel* and *Laughing Water*. In my teens I was lucky enough to be asked to crew in the *Freya*. Sadly, today none of these well loved boats feature in modern regattas but, fortunately, visitors and locals alike can see some of them preserved at the Boat Haven in Unst.

Land sports in the afternoon took place in the Burn Park, just opposite Sellafirth Public Hall. For the young (and not so young) these included sack-races, egg-and-spoon races as well as one-hundred-yard dashes and high jump. No performances were to Olympic standard, but no less entertaining for all that. The main attraction for small boys had to be the motorcycle trials on a course set out around the park. This, of course, was still in the days when Shetland men were finding employment in the Antarctic whaling trade. It was common practice for returning whalers to buy motorcycles en-route home and show them off in the trials course. Motocross it certainly wasn't; great fun it certainly was.

At da hall

Sellafirth Hall was where local lasses cooked 'denner' between the morning and afternoon programmes for crews sailing in the regatta. In the evening everyone would gather for prize-giving to be followed by the regatta concert and dance. The concert was very much of variety in nature, showing off a variable range of local talent in both music and song, interspaced with comic sketches and rhyme often inspired by local events. When the concert had finished, long wooden seating forms would be arranged along the inside perimeter of the hall to leave the floor clear for dancing. With the light now fading, double burner Tilley lamps were lowered by pulleys from the roof, primed, lit and hoisted aloft again. The wooden floor was swept, then prepared by sprinkling on liberal quantities of Slipperine dance floor powder. A band of local musicians, usually with fiddles, accordion and guitar, would gather on the small stage at one end of the hall. Sometimes this could be an impromptu band of individuals carrying or borrowing instruments, a bit of conversation among them and instrument tuning would ensue, then the dance would begin.

Dancing back then was strictly Scottish Country, no jiving to Elvis or rocking around the clock to Bill Haley. Through the night there would be a plethora of common dances everybody knew, such as the Boston Two Step, Gay Gordons and St Bernard's Waltz; these would be interspaced by energy-burning, thirst-inducing, and longer set dances like the Eightsome Reel, Dashing White Sergeant and Circassian Circle. Although never considered as formal occasions, lasses wore frocks and men suits, shirts and ties, with Brylcream almost obligatory on men's hair. No midnight or one o'clock finishes here either; dancing would end as the sun was rising again, between three or four in the morning. The only break dance in those days happened about midnight when the band would stop, Tilley lamps were lowered and pumped up, more forms brought in and everyone seated for a round of tea and sandwiches. A variety of sandwiches and bannocks for all had been prepared in the hall kitchen and volunteers would then carry these on trays to serve the seated dancers. Cups were distributed. Tea had been brewed in, sweetened or not, then poured from, industrial sized kettles by helpers circling the hall calling out "Sugary?" and "Sugarless?" or "Milky tae! I'll fetch de black tae in a meenit." All tastes were catered for at the regatta dance.

No bar or alcohol licence for village halls in those days. Men requiring something more than "sugary tae" to invigorate the dancing muscles retired to the cloakroom. Here, half-bottles of Johnnie Walker or Black and White whisky would appear as if by a magician's hand from inside smart suits to be passed around. Outside, men would seek fresh air in the semi-darkness and yarn, faces familiar and 'uncan' illuminated by the red glow of a cigarette or the flare of a match. In the days before the introduction of canned beer, screw-top glass bottles of India Pale Ale and the like were the standard refresher for the socially thirsty. Later, piles of discarded empties left outside the hall were to be a source of funds to supplement pocket money of those who could gather and return the empties.

The hall was the venue for all our social events. Wedding receptions followed by dances were great occasions. Traditionally, several households in the community would be asked to "take a table" for the reception. In this they would supply food, plates and utensils for the guests to be seated at the table. The "table" would make all the bread, bannocks and other home-bakes; sometimes home-kill mutton too, cooked specially for the event. The Christmas Tree party for the bairns, with a concert and dance, was also held in our hall; sadly depopulation of Sellafirth saw the end of this by 1959 as families left the island.

A winter pastime in many community halls was (and still is in a few) the sport of badminton, with the court lines painted onto the hall floors. Sellafirth had many keen players and there was fierce competition between all the village halls on the island. Halls were lit by the Tilley pressure lamps suspended from the ceiling and it wasn't uncommon for a wayward shuttlecock to take out the occasional lamp mantle.

Another winter pastime that everyone at home, and almost everyone outside Shetland, has heard of is Lerwick's pseudo-Viking, Up-Helly-A' fire festival, held on the last Tuesday in January. Lesser known are the smaller, and much more homely, parish Up-Helly-A's held throughout the winter. For the uninitiated these festivals revolve around the ceremonial burning of a replica Viking galley after a torchlight procession through the village. Squads of villagers in fancy dress (called guizers) perform in the village halls at the dance following the burning.

In 1956 two of my Sellafirth neighbours, Angus and Alistair (both a little older than me), were building a galley out of wooden fish boxes and asked neighbour Robbie a' Dester (Robert Williamson) for some wood. Instead of wood he gave them an old boat to burn and that Sellafirth bairn's Up-Helly-A' was the first to be held in North Yell. The following year the adults got in on the act and a full blown event was organised. Peter Spence of Gutcher was appointed as Guizer Jarl; a galley was built by Robbie and named *Nornagest*. I remember us accompanying the blue and yellow galley, flying the raven banner, with Jarl Peter onboard,

46   A TOWN CALLED TOILETS

as it was pulled from Sellafirth crossroads in a torch-lit procession uphill to the burning site in Portland Quarry. Here Peter jumped out and the blazing torches were thrown in, creating, what seemed to me back then, a most enormous firestorm. Everyone was 'guized-up', their costumes lit up by the fiery glow against the black of the night as they stood around the blazing galley singing the *Norseman's Home*. Signal flares and fireworks followed the song to light up the night sky. I've been to and taken part in many Up-Helly-A' events in Lerwick but

Nornagest, Sellafirth UHA galley; 1957. Photo © Alan and Sunniva Leask.

none can match the excitement and spectacle of my first "grown-up" Up-Helly-A' in Sellafirth.

Following the burning everyone packed into the Sellafirth Hall, almost everyone seemed to be guized-up; I was wearing a cowboy outfit. Some guizers were organised into squads and performed acts; my father, with blackened face, long silk robe and turban, was in a squad of Indian pedlars attempting to sell their wares from suitcases. After the acts tea and sandwiches were served in the traditional manner. The stage at the far end of the hall was then prepared and the Cullivoe Concert Party entertained us. A dance followed but I was tucked up in bed long before then.

Da 'picters' and da 'wireless'

The fortnightly highlight for me was when the hall became our cinema. On a Friday evening a van with Highland and Islands Film Guild emblazoned on its sides would arrive at the hall. Driven by the projectionist and his son, it contained all the essentials to show the latest film that had been advertised for the last week or so in the post office. The van carried a generator to power the projectors that were set up in the men's cloakroom and pointed through small hatches in the wall at the portable screen standing on the hall stage. Seating was the long wooden forms arranged across the middle of the hall, perhaps not as comfortable as a city Odeon, but no less enjoyable. On light summer evenings blackout blinds kept our cinema dark; on snowy winter nights paraffin heaters did little to raise the temperature within the hall so we would wear as many sweaters as could fit under a duffle-coat and as many socks as our feet could stuff into wellie-boots.

The Guild showed most of the well-known feature films of the day, sometimes even before the cinema chains on the mainland. The projectionist in Yell owned a cine camera and filmed local events such as the regatta day; these would sometimes be shown, often causing much amusement or embarrassment if you had been caught on camera. Typically an evening programme started with a Pathe Newsreel followed by cartoons such as Tom & Jerry, Looney Tunes and Merrie Melodies. Usually there would be a short film such as comedy from The Three Stooges or an Edgar Lustgarten *Scotland Yard* crime story. The main feature would follow and then a trailer for the next film. The programme would always end with the National Anthem which everyone respectfully waited and stood for. Standing for the duration of the anthem had the added benefit of helping to restore circulation to the limbs after two hours sitting on a hard wooden seat.

The Highland and Islands Film Guild mobile cinemas provided many, like me, with their first experience of "the movies" and national and international news on film; sometimes there would be short documentaries telling us about other cultures in far flung parts of the Empire. The first feature film I remember seeing was when I was about five years old. This was the Disney film *Davy Crockett, King of the Wild Frontier*, the theme song of which was sung endlessly by small boys for years afterwards.

A year or two later another film was shown that I remember, mainly, because I was not allowed to see it; *The Battle of the River Plate*. I guess the horrors of war were too recent in the minds of my parents for a six year old to be allowed to watch it. I have seen it a few times since on Sunday afternoon TV and its depictions of the horrors of war are mild indeed when compared to the graphic depictions of blood and gore in modern war films. A few years later I was judged old enough to be allowed to see *Sink the Bismarck!* The screening was made even more memorable by the knowledge that the man sitting behind me had been on one of the ships that had engaged the *Bismarck*. I wondered at the time what he thought of the film but I suppose he might not have appreciated being questioned about the battle by a ten year old.

Sadly, depopulation ended Sellafirth's Friday night at 'da picters' in the early 1960s. The Guild continued to show films in the larger settlement of Mid Yell, so a trip to the picters in my early to mid teens was a bicycle ride to the hall there, a round trip of 18 miles! The spread of TV across the Highlands and Islands saw attendances fall and eventually the Guild ceased operation in the early 1970s.

Compared to today the advancement of communication technology was slow. In 1960 we had a telephone installed but this was on a party line with other households: to take a call you were first contacted by the exchange by counting the number of rings; in our case four. Daily news and other entertainment came via a long and medium waveband radio. Not having mains power, the first radio I remember was a valve set in a wooden cabinet powered by a combination of lead-acid accumulator and a large dry battery. The accumulator was periodically recharged by a local crofter who had small aero-generator, so we always kept a charged spare to use when the other was charging. However, a new dry battery had to be purchased occasionally, so the radio was used, almost sparingly, just to listen to specific programmes, not as a continuous background noise like today. Daily broadcasts of *Children's Hour* were followed by the six o'clock news. The weekly hour of Scottish dance music on the BBC Scottish Home Service was always tuned in to. The BBC Light Programme on Sunday mornings had *Family Favourites* request programme and in the afternoon brought programmes like *The Clitheroe Kid*, *The Navy Lark* and *Round the Horne*.

On winter evenings when reception was better we'd tune into Radio Luxemburg or American Forces Network. Some Radio Luxemburg programmes were sponsored by Horace Bachelor to promote his "Famous Infra-Draw Method" of predicting results for football pools entries and collecting stake monies from the gullible hopeful. My father, who did a Littlewoods football pool coupon every week, reckoned that if the Infra-Draw Method was so infallible Bachelor wouldn't need to take money from the punters to make a living.

Whalers returning from South Georgia revolutionised radio listening for many in Shetland. They shared accommodation with Norwegians who were equipped with very good quality portable transistor radios powered by torch batteries. Very soon these started appearing in Shetland households, imported from Norway via South Georgia. A whaler neighbour acquired one for my father in the early 1960s. Using this radio was my first step into the modern age of broadcast technology. Even so I could rarely get good reception from the pirate radio ship Radio Caroline; better reception came from the Dutch ship Radio Veronica. My parents were most definitely not fans of sixties pop culture emanating from these stations. Radio Scotland was also a pirate radio ship that I tuned into for a year or two until it closed in 1967; output from this station was much superior to that offered by present day BBC Radio Scotland.

'Atween' da 'brods'

Detailed news came via newspapers. These we ordered from the Sellafirth shop, and when it closed, through the sub-post office. Local news came through two weekly broadsheet newspapers: *The Shetland News* on Thursday; *The Shetland Times* on Saturday. Not surprisingly, given our remoteness and limitations of transport to the island, there was no delivery of daily newspapers. To overcome this problem we subscribed to the weekly edition of *The Overseas Daily Mirror* in which a whole week's papers were bound into a single volume. This was back in the days when newspapers like the *Mirror* were serious conveyors of news and analysis; so unlike the purveyors of trivia and sensationalised activities of the shallow lives of glitterati, footballers and minor royals that tabloid papers have evolved into.

Other weeklies I remember were the *Sunday Post* and *Weekly News*. I read them all, thanks to my grandfather probably starting me reading at an age much younger than my level of understanding of national and international events. I did like to follow the strip cartoons such as the adventures of 'Garth' and 'The Perishers' in the *Mirror*, and of course 'Oor Wullie' and 'The Broons' in the *Sunday Post*. 'The Perishers' appealed to my developing strange sense of humour. I loved all the characters, especially the crabs in the rock pool. These crabs had developed an entire religion around the annual appearance on his seaside holiday of Boot (the Old English sheepdog) who stares down into their pool. I loved the depiction of the annual mystic visitation of "Eyeballs in the Sky" and the ensuing conflict between the views of the preacher crab and the scientist crab resulting in crab-wars. So much of our human condition was brilliantly reflected by the crabs in the rock pool; "Eek!"

I wasn't into comics in a big way, I didn't get the *Dandy* or the *Beano* but I did take slightly more believable *Victor* and *Hotspur* for a few years. I did try the *Boy's Own Paper*, but tired of it after a while, feeling that it didn't have much relevance to a crofter's son growing up in a remote Shetland island. I much preferred my father's monthly magazines, *Wide World* and *Reader's Digest*. The *Wide World* had great photographs and artwork as well as stories; *The Times* once described *Wide World* stories thus: "brave chaps with large moustaches on stiff upper lips, who did stupid and dangerous things".

What I did discover, and collect through mail order, was *Classics Illustrated*; classic stories in literature presented in comic strip style with fantastic artwork.

These were condensed versions of the stories and a great incentive to read the original books such as *Moby Dick* and *A Tale of Two Cities* from the library. The primary and secondary schools I went to in Yell had libraries which it operated on behalf of Zetland County Public Library. My father was also an avid reader so I withdrew books each week on his behalf, and read them as well. I also started a collection of paperback novels from an unusual source: for a while our twice weekly Co-op grocery van sold cans of soft drinks with promotional tokens on them; if I collected six tokens I could send these off and get a paperback. In this way I became a fan of Ian Fleming's James Bond stories.

Sent-errands and star-struck

Occasional trips to Lerwick offered me a chance to buy more paperbacks from bookshops in Lerwick. Although we never considered ourselves as such, by today's standards we would have been looked on as remote from nearly all that civilisation had to offer. Back then there were two ways in which to take a 'vaege' to "da toon". One option was a small cargo and passenger vessel that served the North Isles from Lerwick three times a week. The *MV Earl of Zetland* brought almost all freight, including animals and vehicles, in and out of the isles of Yell, Unst, Fetlar, Whalsay and Out Skerries, so wasn't the quickest way to get to and from Lerwick. The introduction of roll-on, roll-off car ferries between all the islands by 1974 replaced the work of the much loved *Earl* and she left Shetland in 1975. The *Earl* is now moored in North Shields and is a floating bar and restaurant.

The second, and quicker option from Sellafirth to Lerwick, was by public service bus to Mid Yell then a connecting bus to Ulsta in the south end of the island. From Ulsta a small passenger ferry, the *Shalder*, crossed Yell Sound to Toft in Mainland; from there another service bus took passengers to Lerwick. Known as the Overland Service, this carried all the mail and newspapers to Yell and onward to Unst via another small ferry, the *Tystie*, that crossed from Gutcher. Another small boat, *Rose*, ran a ferry service from Mid Yell to Fetlar. A return journey from home to Lerwick on the same day was only possible in the summer months, and then only on Tuesdays and Saturdays. For me a vaege to Lerwick by the Overland took four hours going (because of numerous stops to pick up outgoing mails at post boxes) and two and a half hours returning in the evening. Today, with much improved roads and fast car ferries plying between the islands, the same vaege takes one and a half hours each way.

In the 1960s Lerwick's main street, Commercial Street, was a far cry from the near ghost town appearance it has today. In those days the "da Street" resembled that of any busy market town with several bakers, butchers, drapers, tailors, knitwear specialists, hardware shops, ironmongers, licensed grocers, ship-chandlers, newsagents, chemists, hotels, bars and cafes all doing good trade, many remaining open well into the evening. In those days the regular cargo and passenger vessels from Aberdeen and Leith discharged at Victoria Pier, just a stone's throw from the shops in the town centre. Just a little further along the

Yell Sound ferry Shalder at Ulsta; 1968. Photo © Shetland Museum.

waterfront was the busy fishmarket, with boats landing their catches. Summer saw the arrival of the herring fleets bringing hundreds of itinerant seasonal workers. On summer Saturdays crews ashore from the herring fleet and seasonal shore workers would throng Lerwick's narrow main street. Joining the hustle and bustle would be folk that had come down on the "Owerlawnd" from the North Isles or by bus from other parts of Shetland shopping and generally having a day in "da Toon".

Over the years technology and overfishing brought the demise of the labour-intensive herring industry and the compulsory EU shrinking of our fishing fleets. This, along with the relocation of the fish market and cargo/passenger terminal well away from the town centre, saw almost all the long established shops close down. Large supermarkets appeared on the outskirts of Lerwick selling all manner of goods and services and these finally reduced "da Street" to a mere shadow of its former self. The unique character of "da Street" was finally killed off in the 1990s by Shetland Islands Council when they removed the historic hand-cut flagstone paving slabs from its entire length. These were a pleasing patchwork of buff, fawn and light grey local sandstone that would reflect a light and cheery atmosphere even on the dullest and wettest of days. The replacement paving, chosen with no sense of history or aesthetics, is a machine cut, uniform dark featureless grey mudstone slab imported from Caithness. This has the remarkable property of turning almost coal black when wet imparting a despairing sense of ghost town decay and gloom to "da Street".

Sometime in my early teens I was allowed to make day trips to Lerwick on my own during the summer holidays. I think that my very first trip to "da Toon" on my own was as a young teenager to buy my own full-sized tushker, as up until then I'd been using a cut down version. My first stop was to visit "Smiler", the blacksmith, who had a reputation for making the finest tushker blades at The

Smithy on Commercial Road. Sadly this distinctive old building was demolished in the 1970s and an important part of Lerwick's history lost. Proudly clutching my tushkar iron with Smiler's "S" signature stamped on the heel I made "in ower" to Jeemie Irvine's hardware shop by the Market Cross to buy a ready-made 'heft' for my new tushker. I would have a list of sent-errands from my father to buy in various shops in Lerwick, mostly from hardware and fishing tackle shops. Once I had gathered all my errands I would leave them with a pile of other folk's property in Jeemie Irvine's hardware shop by the Market Cross. The corner, just inside the shop door, was Lerwick's unofficial left-luggage, no guards, no lockers, no keys, no tickets, no checking in and out; everybody just accepted that what you left there all day would still be there when you came to collect it. Changed days.

A week or so before one of my sent-errand trips to Lerwick, the film *Tunes of Glory* starring Alec Guinness and John Mills had been shown in the Sellafirth Hall. I had been hoping for a war film along the lines of *Ice Cold in Alex*. I didn't really get into the dark psychological drama played out by Guinness and Mills, but the picture was much brightened by the brief appearance of an attractive young actress as the Major's daughter. Returning from Lerwick on that particular trip an attractive young lady boarded the passenger ferry for the crossing of Yell Sound. To me she seemed the spitting image of the actress in the film, but of course it couldn't be. I must have been unashamedly staring at her on the ferry crossing, but when we boarded the bus at Ulsta she smiled at me and said hello. A few miles up the road she spoke to the driver and he let her off, whereupon she started walking down a side road towards some houses. Only years later did I discover that the young lady had a relative living on Yell, and was indeed the young actress in the film, Susannah York. I had been star-struck.

Another memorable Overland trip was when I was in my late teens going to Lerwick to catch the overnight ferry to Aberdeen. The ferry to and from Aberdeen, then and now, is colloquially known as the "Nort Boat" (after the old North of Scotland Orkney & Shetland Steam Navigation Company aka "the North Company") or just "da Boat". This was in mid-winter with a lot of snow on the ground and not without some difficulty the mail-bus had made it through the single track roads of Yell to Ulsta. I was the only Overland passenger that day. When I got off the ferry at Toft the bus for Lerwick was waiting to collect the mails and me. As was the custom I helped the ferry crew and the bus driver to load the mail bags onto the bus.

The driver of that route for many years was the much esteemed Freddie, renowned for his dry sense of humour. On boarding the bus Freddie tells me that the main road to Lerwick is blocked by a 'fan' at the notorious Dales Lees and we are to use an alternative route via the single track road along the shore of Sullom Voe to Brae and by Olna Firth to rejoin the main road at Voe. Although the wind was picking up, causing some 'bearin' of lying snow, everything goes well until we reach Mulla, on the outskirts of Voe. Here a fan has formed across the road and it is obvious that the bus won't get through without some physical assistance. We both get out of the bus and look at the build-up of snow. Freddie pushes his flat cap back, takes out a cigarette, lights it, looks me up and down, opens the luggage compartment and takes out a large shovel. "Is du wantin ta catch da boat da night?" he says.

"Yis," says I.

He hands me the shovel. "Dere du is, hit'll no tak dee lang ta dell wis trowe!"

'Haddin oot a langer'

In complete contrast to long hours of summer daylight, Shetland winter days are short and nights are long and dark. In the days before mains electricity brought TV and the decline of normal social interaction, neighbours would drop by of an evening to "hadd wis oot a langer"; this by yarning about everything and anything. Conversation could be local news, or retelling of experiences from sailing and whaling days, or stories from generations back, or folklore. In her later years my mother would often wish that she'd listened to the auld folk yarning when she was young and remembered more. Today in writing this, I wish exactly the same.

One item of family folklore that sometimes came up was of a dream that mother's maternal grandmother had. At the time, she was living with her husband Robert and their large family at the croft of Uncadal (later to be evicted by John Walker), where one of the family was ill with jaundice. She dreamt that if she went to a certain place in the nearby hills she would find a shell. With this shell and a wooden bowl she was to form a specific ritual of collecting water in the bowl and cause the patient to drink the water from the shell. She did as she was bidden and found the shell and followed the ritual, thus curing the patient.

This 'shall' and the accompanying 'kapp' were supposed to have come from the mythical 'hill-folk' also known as the 'trows' in Shetland. Both were lent out together to be used as a cure for 'gulsa' in the community. Eventually both were given to my grandmother for safekeeping then passed down to my mother. Following her death, I donated them to Shetland Museum where they are on display; (see *Excursus 3. Da Gulsa Shall and da Trowie Kapp*).

Reddin up kin

Redding up kin was a favourite topic of these evening visits. Today our tourist industry is boosted by the descendants of Shetland expatriates returning to explore their roots, the modern form of redding up kin. In my family tree, on my mother's side, two Urquhart brothers, supposedly pipers, arrived in Shetland from Scotland via Orkney after the failure of the 1745 rebellion, presumably having been on the losing Jacobite side. Nisbets may well have arrived in Shetland in the 16th century as servants to the black-hearted Sheriff of Zetland, Laurence Bruce of Cultmalindie, builder of Muness Castle in Unst. The Fraser side of the family in Shetland goes back to about 1740, supposedly descended from a shipwreck survivor.

Further back my ancestral tree spreads ever outwards, complicated by the Norse tradition of patronymic names, a common practice in Shetland before the 19th century. Like many Shetlanders my family tree also branches into Sinclairs and Stewarts, the Scots landowners and Earls of Shetland and Orkney, thereby back (on both sides of the blanket) through the royal gene-pools of Scotland and England. Some were good and some were pretty awful; one of my favourite distant ancestors by this reckoning is Elizabeth Woodville, mother of the Princes in the Tower.

My mother had three siblings: her older sister May who married an English soldier in WW2; an older brother John, and a younger brother William. William pursued a career at sea and became a master mariner and a ship owner; tragically he was knocked down by a car outside his home in Kirkcaldy and died at the age of sixty-two.

I remember my mother recalling a curious happening that befell her older brother who had also followed the family tradition of sailing. When home on leave John had bicycled the seven miles to a dance in Cullivoe, North Yell. On the single track road between Cullivoe and Gutcher there is small bridge that crosses the burn outflow from the Loch of Garth into the sea. He would cycle across this on the way to the dance. The next day he confided a strange tale to my mother. He told her that on his way back from the dance, when he came to the bridge he felt that he couldn't cross it. To get to the other side of the burn he carried his bicycle all the way around the loch so not to cross the bridge and rejoined the road at the far side. This was to be John's last leave home from sea; tragically on his next voyage he drowned in the harbour of Antwerp in 1935.

Superstition was always part of the Shetland psyche. After an evening's visiting, the traditional parting words of the host to the guests would often be, "So geng you, an His Blissins be wi you." To which would come a reply of qualified optimism, "We'll see you ageen, if we're spared."

Left: Uncle John Urquhart; 1935. Right: Uncle Captain William D.N. Urquhart.

Fit the Fourth: Educating Allen

Education is what remains after one has forgotten what one has learned in school.

So said Albert Einstein, and who am I to argue. I can't say that I disliked school, that doesn't mean to say I liked it overmuch either. I liked studying from books more than the school processes. Some lessons I loved and some I hated, other lessons I would have loved to have loved, but any enthusiasm for those was dispelled by poor teachers. Despite the best efforts of schools' careers service to advise the contrary, I left school for college and much later went on to do an honours degree with the Open University.

Gutcher schooldays

Memories of my first day at school are a bit of a haze. Suffice to say I didn't enjoy it overmuch. Because of my late autumn birthday I started school after the 1955 summer holidays, before reaching the mandatory age of five years. The outcome of this early start was that for the rest of my schooling I would be a school year ahead of many others of the same age. Later this caused complications when I approached school leaving age.

My first primary school was at Gutcher overlooking Blue Mull Sound, the stretch of water between Yell and Unst. The school was exactly a two-mile walk from where the Wasterhoose track joined the main road. If the track into Wasterhoose had been allowed to be taken into account then walking distance would be more than two miles and school transport would have been provided. The main road at that time was a single track, metalled affair with numerous potholes that climbed the hill past Sellafirth Hall, then wound its way through the gentle slopes of moor-covered hills past Sand Water Loch to Gutcher. Ten of us walked to school from Sellafirth on my first day, a happy bunch we were too;

Gutcher school pupils; 1957. Back row: Agnes Williamson; Cathleen Jamieson; Yvonne Bayes; Kathleen Brown; Ruth Ramsay; Masie Brown. Front row: Bert Ramsay; Alistair Jamieson; Hunter Jamieson; Allen Fraser; Angus Jamieson; Jim Ramsay.

at the school another two joined us, making a grand total of twelve. Tarmac was only laid on that stretch of road about three years later.

Fortunately it was just the terms immediately before and after the summer holidays that we were required to walk to school; the education authority laid on transport for us during the winter terms. A crofter from North Sandwick was hired to provide our winter transport, which was handy as his family also attended the school. Jeemie was a gentleman in every sense of the word. He drove us in a flat-nosed Morris van fitted with seating in the back for his passengers. If there was a down side, it was that Jeemie was a pipe smoker and he always lit up after picking up the last pupils. By the time we'd rattled and bumped the two miles to school all the occupants in the back were having a 'Condor moment'. Passive smoking didn't exist in the 1950s.

Twelve pupils and one teacher: three in my class, two in the class above, four in the one above that, and three in the top class (if memory serves me right). Three of the possible seven classes had no pupils. We sat in our straight rows of front-facing, metal-framed, two-seater, oak desks looking toward the teacher at her table and the blackboard on its stand. These were real desks; the ones with the fold up seats, lift-up lids, slate-slots, pen-holders and inkwells, all exhibiting many generations of ink stains and doodles, scratches and carved initials.

The floor was bare wood floorboards. Windows at the back behind the desks looked out onto the grassy playground. Against the wall, to the right of the entrance door, stood giant glass-fronted bookcases that held the books of the public library. These also held school materials along with plasticine and wooden educational toys, which we loved. On the opposite side of the room towards the front was a pot-bellied stove for heating. Fuel for the stove was provided by the generosity of the Education Authority; in my mother's time pupils had to carry peats for the stove to school with them each day.

On the wall behind the teacher, hung yellowing maps of the world stretched between ebony rods above and below. Much of the landmasses were in fading pink, by then fading in tandem with the glory of the British Empire the colour once depicted. On the front window ledge, to the right of the teacher, stood a white enamelled jug of water and a mug. Anyone needing a drink raised a hand, asked permission by including the words "Please, Miss, may I?" A similar procedure was followed to get rid of the water again. High on the wall, above the teacher's head, hung a large plaque with a copper cross bearing a long list of names that I often stared at and wondered about. In time I discovered these were the names of former pupils who gave their lives in World War One.

Attached to the schoolroom were the school teacher's residence and the school canteen for school dinners. The canteen was the domain of Annie, the resident cook. A kinder soul there never was. Once a week as a special treat she made ice-cream using the paraffin-powered fridge-freezer in the little kitchen. The morning break was also the milk break. Someone, somewhere, had decreed that a school full of crofter children, who practically lived on milk and butter, needed extra milk at the morning break. Not fresh cow's milk, but dried milk powder which had to be mixed with water and boiled up on a stove. This disgusting brew was served up in pastel-coloured Bakelite tumblers. Apart from the awful taste, this milk, however hot, had the remarkable physical characteristic of immediately congealing a thick, off-yellow skin on top. This skin had an inherent property of unfailingly attaching itself to the upper lip of anyone drinking it. Once attached it would hang down like a vile curtain of snot; if the taste wasn't enough to make you 'byock', then the visual presence of your neighbour so decorated certainly was.

Our teacher was of the old school (pun not intended). Respected, strict, but not always fair, she did seem to have it in for one pupil who had difficulty reading (not me). My problem when I started school was that I always replied to her in my best Shetland dialect, much to her extreme annoyance. It took her some considerable time to break me of this habit and force me to use only Queen's English in the classroom. In fact, use of Shetland dialect was strictly forbidden in the classroom all through my primary and secondary schooldays. If we spoke in 'wir midder tongue' in class we got severely told off. Back in my mother's time the penalty for this was a thrashing.

Denigration of our dialect by our educationalists was quite an astonishing psychological crime against our culture, especially as during my schooldays most teachers were native Shetlanders. Perhaps this harks back to earlier generations when formal schooling began and many teachers were imported Scots. Back then our education providers saw our rich Shetland dialect as being inferior; its use would hold us back educationally, stifle our mental development and lessen our chances of employment. Thanks to well over a century of educational repression, our spoken dialect, the last vestige of our Norse heritage, is in terminal decline along with its rich variety of twangs from each Shetland parish. Even today this ingrained sense of inferiority persists when some native Shetlanders, such as teachers, local politicians or presenters on local radio, feel it necessary to 'knapp' and mispronounce Shetland place-names despite their audience still being predominantly dialect speakers.

Strange to think that over sixty years ago I wrote my first words at school on a tablet and today I'm writing much of this book on a tablet. The very first educational materials I was given at Gutcher School were a slate and a slate pencil, the slate being about the same size as my tablet computer today. In fact I was given my mother's old slate that her brother John had carved her initials on. Learning to form letters correctly on a slate and later with pen and ink encouraged the habit of a copperplate style of writing; sadly a habit that I lost many years later.

School lessons were pretty much standard primary school fare of the three Rs, history and geography with a bit of soul salvation thrown in. The latter being the morning recitation of the Lord's Prayer and an occasional visit from a Church of Scotland minister. On one occasion we even had a visit from no less a person than Moderator of the General Assembly of the Church of Scotland. The only thing I remember about his visit was him showing off the ring he was wearing, and that it held a violet stone engraved with the burning bush symbol.

In the playground we went through the usual repertoire of children's games; rounders was a favourite. Over the next five years older pupils left and fewer new pupils joined due to continued depopulation of the island. Within five years of my starting school the school roll had fallen from twelve to two and in 1960 the school closed.

The long hot summer

The year that the road was tarmacked around Basta Voe to Sellafirth and on to Gutcher was a memorable one. During our school summer holiday we would often hitch rides in the lorry cabs running to and from the tarmac-making plant in Cullivoe. All the drivers were kind and amazingly tolerant of small boys' chatter and questions about different lorry types, whether they were petrol or diesel, Bedford or Leyland. Those lorries were old, with scratched and faded windscreens, worn metal dashboards, switches held in place by clothes-pegs, torn leather seats, cabs full of diesel fumes mingled with the smell of hot oil, bitumen and cigarette smoke. They rattled and banged along at a bone-jarring

50 mph when empty, but struggled to make 20 mph uphill with a full load as gears crashed and transmissions whined in protest. We loved them.

Hot tarmac was tipped by the trucks onto the prepared, metalled road surface. The road-men would attack the smoking hot piles of black, bitumen-covered stones with metal forks and wheelbarrows, then spread it out evenly with forks and metal rakes. Next, our favourite vehicle arrived to finish the job: the huge, British-racing-green road-roller rumbled into position with its large spinning flywheel and tall chimney-exhaust. We all envied the driver in his high seat turning an overlarge steering wheel to direct the huge, barrel front roller as he chugged forwards and backwards over a strip of hot tarmac, steaming from the water sprays on the roller. With the seemingly frenzied activity, the heat, the smoke, the steam and the smell, we felt part of the white heat of our own industrial revolution. Even today a whiff of hot tarmac takes me right back to that wondrous, long, hot summer.

Mid Yell schooldays

With the closure of Gutcher School I was assigned to Mid Yell Primary School, some nine miles away. Each morning I caught Jamieson's school bus that took pupils from Cullivoe to Mid Yell Junior Secondary on the same site. Along with the North Yell pupils, the bus collected pupils from the settlements of Basta and North-a-Voe. I doubt if there was ever a more cheerful school bus anywhere; there was never a dull moment with almost continuous good-natured banter between the passengers and the driver, Jeems John, one of nature's natural jokers. Happy days.

The classes at my new school were somewhat larger than at Gutcher. This was a two-teacher primary with the younger pupils in a separate classroom. For the next two years of my primary education we had a first-class teacher who projected a fairly laid back approach to teaching, but in fact was getting the very best he could out of his pupils. After two years I progressed into secondary education after sitting the so called eleven-plus exam.

In those days there was a choice of secondary education depending on eleven-plus exam results. Those who passed could go to the Anderson Educational Institute in Lerwick from the age of twelve to pursue an academic route for six more years, then perhaps on to university. For pupils from the North Isles this option required living away from home for the whole of each school term until they left school. Boarding accommodation was provided in school hostels managed by the education authority. The Overland service didn't operate on Friday afternoons or on Sunday evenings, so for North Isles pupils there was no option to get home at weekends; effectively this educational choice meant you had flown the nest at the age of eleven or twelve. At this age a child from the North Isles wouldn't see home again for a full term. He or she would be plunged into an alien environment of much larger classes with less teacher attention in a school and hostel rife with systemic bullying. The other choice was to follow a more vocational route of four years of secondary education at a local Junior Secondary School or at the Lerwick Central School. The latter offered more courses than the local JS schools but also required leaving home to lodge in the school hostel. If you failed the eleven-plus then it was a case of the local JS or Lerwick Central for the next four years.

I can't remember taking the eleven-plus, but I suppose I must have done. The result would have been immaterial anyway. Being a school year ahead of my age my parents weren't keen on me leaving home to live in the hostel at the young age of eleven, and I don't think I was too keen on the idea either. In any event, my next four years of education was to be growing up on the croft and joining the happy bus to attend Mid Yell Junior Secondary School. Mid Yell JS School offered a curriculum of English, history, geography, arithmetic, mathematics, science and art, but only the first four to Scottish O-level standard. In addition to this there was a strong vocational curriculum of navigation/seamanship, woodwork/metalwork and domestic science delivered by itinerant teachers who worked a circuit of JS schools. The rationale behind this was that school leavers would be more likely to remain in the community with these vocational skills at a time when rates of unemployment and depopulation were high.

Apart from the headmaster, the teachers at Mid Yell were as good as you could wish for. They knew their pupils, took an interest in their work and progress and always commanded interest with good humour. This attitude produced good results; well in me it did anyway. What a contrast from the headmaster who taught arithmetic and maths in the secondary school as well as music in the primary school. He used the FBI method of running the school and delivering lessons, that is Fear, Bullying and Intimidation. I first encountered him at primary school music class. Although I loved music and can easily carry a tune in my head, I have no resemblance of a singing voice whatsoever, so would generally mime my way through class singing. Our headmaster/music teacher would soon notice anyone doing this and any non-conformist singer would be hauled out in front and humiliated by being made to perform solo.

His arithmetic and maths classes were held under the same cloak of fear; no-one would dare ask a question to clarify some point. If a pupil was asked a question and didn't grasp the point being put across it was bad news. He was in the habit of standing that pupil out in front of the class and repeating the point until the correct answer was given. Failure to grasp the point often resulted in the pupil being repeatedly jabbed hard inside the shoulder by the clenched joint of the forefinger, sometimes vigorously enough to propel the pupil across the room. He wasn't afraid to use the tawse which he carried slung over his shoulder inside his jacket. During exams he would pace up and down between desks looking over pupils' shoulders. Not surprisingly perhaps, I didn't do well in those exams.

I had great classmates at Mid Yell and some great teachers, but at the end of the day I was glad when I completed my fourth year and could leave. Therein lay a problem; having started school early I was still only fifteen, with no job prospect and, in reality, crofting wasn't going to offer me a living. Although I'd not exactly excelled at arithmetic and maths, I enjoyed navigation classes and seamanship lessons. Our itinerant teacher in these subjects was a retired sea-captain, Frank Laurenson, who now lived in Sellafirth. Originally from West Burrafirth in Mainland, he'd acquired a taste for rabbit and 'scarf' (which he curried), and for a small fee I would supply him with both. He had strongly recommended a sea-going career to me, and with a family history of sailing, this was now much in my mind.

On leaving school I would have liked to have gone to college prior to starting a merchant navy career as an apprentice, but I was still too young. I did propose crewing on a fishing boat for a year or two, but my mother was dead set against that for the understandable reason that there had been a spate of recent fishing tragedies. I suggested to the education authority's careers guidance that I do Highers in English, history and geography to add to my O-levels in those subjects. This, I thought, I could do at the Anderson Institute in fifth year. For some reason, which I never really understood, this was deemed not possible and I was advised to repeat a fourth year at Lerwick Central with my academic peers and then do a fifth year at the Anderson.

Lerwick Central School

Lerwick Central was not a railway station as the name might suggest, but it might as well have been for all the educational value I got out of it. When I arrived there I very soon found out that because I had already done a fourth year, I was an educational misfit as far as the school was concerned. School timetables and classes were organised by which section you were assigned to - Technical or Commercial. I would have preferred to be assigned to the Technical timetable because that would have given me navigation classes, which I had liked at Mid Yell. The school had assigned me to the Commercial timetable to enable a follow-on fifth year at the Anderson, so I had to stick with that, like it or not.

I didn't get off to a good start. My first class was O-level English, which I had already passed. I had mistakenly assumed that I could also sit a Higher at this school; I was wrong. I explained to the teacher that I already passed the English O-level. His response was "What are you doing in my class then!" This was a statement, not a question, and I don't think he ever spoke to me again for the rest of the year. I soon discovered that attitude was pretty much par for the course for the whole school. Never once did I see a teacher encourage a pupil. On the other side there seemed to be little respect shown for most of the teachers, who were often mocked behind their backs. Staff just went through the motions of teaching pupils, who they seemed to regard as no more than simple fodder for the local labour market at the end of the year. This was either the first or second year of a new headmaster for this school and he just hadn't got to grips with the job, or improved the quality of the educational output, nor had he gained the respect of the pupils.

For my year in Lerwick the school hostel was full, so I was farmed out to lodge in approved digs with an elderly couple in St Sunniva Street. I was very lucky to be staying there, for kinder and more tolerant hosts would have been hard to find, although my bedroom was small and not handy for studying. Another upside of my year in Lerwick was that I met up with one of my neighbours from Sellafirth who had moved to Lerwick when the Gutcher School closed. I also made a number of new friends; a few years later a chance meeting with one in particular was to set me off in a career direction that I had never contemplated. Next to the Central School was Islesburgh Youth Hostel that also ran a youth club and cafe and was open most evenings. Harold, the manager, and Zegena, who served in the cafe, did more to support and advise youngsters than anyone from the school.

Near the end of the school year the education authority's careers officer made his advisory visits to set pupils off on their way in the big bad world. Once again this was a "going through the motions" exercise. I was offered no real encouragement in my desire to go to Merchant Navy College, this apparently because I was in Commercial classes. He didn't deem me suitable for a fifth year at the Anderson so he merely suggested I look for a shop job locally. In his pile of leaflets I'd found one on the Forestry Commission so my response was to ask if he could arrange for me to have a career as a tree surgeon in Shetland. I never heard from him again. I wonder why? Once exams were over I had no wish to waste more of my life there by staying until the end of the school year. I left.

Granite City

Back home from Lerwick, I applied directly to Robert Gordon's Institute of Technology, School of Navigation in Aberdeen for a course as a Merchant Navy cadet deck officer, and was accepted. I applied to Shetland's educational authority for a bursary to cover books and accommodation, which was granted. My mother taught me to iron shirts, my father showed me how to darn socks, and then I was ready to go. After a short summer of casting and 'hurling' paets to earn some extra money I was on my way to the Granite City along with three other Shetland lads on the same course.

Our accommodation was in the Sailors Home in dockside Mearns Street. This was home from home to students at the School as well as accommodation for merchant seamen looking for a ship, or just passing through. The study bedrooms were a delight compared to the cramped bedroom in my Lerwick digs. The food was good and plentiful, the staff kind and helpful, and there was a large television lounge with a dartboard. Upstairs on the way to the bedrooms was a small library and the port chaplain's office should a soul require his services. The canteen/cafe was open most of the time and was a good social centre to sit and yarn with colleagues. Here too we could glean information from other lads who had gone through their cadetship at sea and were now studying for their 'tickets'.

Sometimes we'd meet an old AB, bosun or ex-whaler who was happy to sit with young prospective ship's officers and regale tales of horror and hardship, probably in attempt to scare their future officers off sailing for life. Some were legends in their own lifetime, some in their own lifestyle. For many, a ship on the sea was their home, ashore was an unnatural place, useful only for the proverbial wine, women and song. One that I remember came from the same island as me. He was a legend among legends and many tales have been told about him. He appeared in the cafe one evening after pub closing time, three sheets to the wind with some other Shetland seamen, where they all sat around a table. Their conversation came around to redding up kin and one asked the legend, "Wharr cam du fae, John?"

He considered for a moment, then leaned forward to peer conspiritively at each of the others in turn through the round, bottle-thick lenses of his spectacles: "My father wis a Rooshin sailor, an my mother a Liverpool hoor!"; then sat back, banged his coffee mug down and roared with laughter.

I last saw John a few years later when I was on a flight from London back to Shetland. I'd changed planes in Glasgow, we'd boarded and were strapped in, we waited for a while then suddenly both stewardesses left the plane and hurried off back to the gate. The pilot announced that we were waiting for a very important passenger. About five minutes later the stewardesses reappeared from the terminal. One was leading a portly man by the arm who appeared to be just a little unsteady on his feet. He was wearing a crumpled grey suit with the jacket unbuttoned to reveal an open-necked white shirt. When they got a bit closer to my window I recognised the bottle-thick glasses and trilby hat pushed back on his head. The other stewardess carried the VIP in a large cage: the biggest green and yellow parrot imaginable. They had a seat each directly behind me, did John and the parrot, and were fussed over by the stewardesses on the whole flight north. I often wondered if the parrot repeated some choice phrases from him and what they were. Those men are all long gone now, they embodied a way of life and a British Merchant Navy that has gone with them. The world is a sadder place for their passing. I'm glad that, although only briefly, I met at least a few of them.

The School of Navigation in King Street was an old building with numerous classrooms in a park setting. Courses were not just for cadets but for those acquiring all officer certificates in the Merchant Navy. There was a boathouse with boats on the river to train us in small-boat handling. For longer trips the School owned the sixty-three-year-old *Radium of Don*, a converted Zulu sailing drifter. We had a few trips in her before she was replaced by the newly-built, sixty-six-foot, steel, two-masted staysail schooner, *T/S Robert Gordon*. The School also had a bothy in the Aboyne area where the course was to spend the odd activity weekend; in today's corporate jargon "team bonding exercises". School lecturers were a pretty amenable bunch who were all approachable and gave their best for a fairly disparate class of fifteen young hopefuls. The Shetland group were the more mature, most having lived away from home, thus were more tuned to a college-type environment compared to the Aberdeen City contingent who still lived at home with their parents. All in all we pretty much got on well together.

We studied hard during the week and partied at the weekends, when cash flow allowed. Still a year or so underage we were never challenged in the bars. Often we'd be in the student bars like the Marischal or the Blue Lamp, other times we'd be in dockside pubs like the National or the Commerce Inn ("or onywye ye like") also known as Peep-Peeps. Aberdeen in those days was still a major distant-water trawler port, so to see dockside life in the raw we'd look into the Moorings or The Stanley Hotel. Davy Jones Locker was a favourite haunt; this cellar bar had ultraviolet lighting that made white clothing glow. To exploit the effect to its maximum, I bought a large, brilliant-white, polo-neck sweater from C&A which I've still got, fifty years on. At this time the Irish folk group The Dubliners were high in the charts with the song *The Black Velvet Band* which was also one of the records on Davy Jones's jukebox. One evening a lad in our company emptied all his loose change into the jukebox, repeatedly selecting just that one song. Thirty minutes later the barman switched it off, and we were on a warning; no more Irish songs to drink to that night.

The deer hunter

One memorable weekend at the Aboyne bothy a group of eight of us were given a map reading and leadership exercise. The plan was that we'd navigate a route that would take us for a long hike through the hills and down to a village where we were to camp for the night. For this we were issued with army surplus rucksacks, groundsheets and tents as well as rations. The group was subdivided into pairs that would map-read to a waypoint before passing on to the next pair. Fortunately the weather was good for it didn't take long for other problems to start. The army surplus kit we were issued with was vintage and extraordinarily heavy, especially as none of us really knew how to pack weight properly for a hike. Two of the lads were not exactly up to carrying the weight and progress got slower. Not only that, but blisters were starting to make their presence felt on erstwhile nautical feet. To help ease the situation some of the stronger lads took to carrying extra kit from the over-laden. Just when I least needed it the webbing on a shoulder strap broke, so everyone had to wait while I repaired it. This I did by cutting holes in the strap and rejoining the two ends by threading and re-threading string through the holes. A couple of miles further on I discovered to my annoyance I'd left my new Cold Finger pocket knife back at the repair site. No way was I going to run back for it, so I guess it'll still be there.

As the day wore on we seemed to be navigating our way along the route okay, but it was becoming increasingly obvious that we were never going to make the campsite by nightfall. Our intended destination was a field by a village kirk where we had been instructed to camp for the night, then we were to walk the few miles back along the road to the bothy the following morning. Navigation in the dark through rough heather, peat bog and unknown hillside wasn't going to be an option. We did consider camping overnight in the glen we were now following. The problem with this was that if we hadn't reached our destination by nightfall a mountain rescue team might be called out, an embarrassment we didn't need. By this time I was sharing leading and map-reading duties with another lad. We were pretty sure of our position, so we worked out that if we left the glen from where we were we could take a short, direct route over the hill to our intended destination.

Our plan B worked out just fine. We climbed the hill out of the glen and crossed a heath-covered plateau where we encountered a stag and several deer heading across our path. They seemed as surprised to see us as we were them and immediately they veered off sharply downhill back towards the glen we'd come from. Soon we could see the village with its kirk and walled graveyard. Our campsite was to be a grassy area just by the kirk wall. With the last of the daylight we had just started to sort out the tents when we heard, then saw, a tractor approaching us at speed down the track to the kirk.

Standing in the tractor link box was a large man dressed in dark tweeds. Even at a distance in the twilight we could see his face was a flushed reddish-purple. Even more impressive than his face colour was the .303 rifle slung over his shoulder. From his demeanour we suspected this was no social call to welcome us to the village. Along with casting aspersions on our collective parentage, our visitor enquired if we were the group that had just crossed the plateau above the village, to which we replied in the affirmative. Embedded in another interesting combination of expletives came information that our route over the hill had totally spoiled (not his words) the deer shoot of Lord (I forget his name) and his guests. Seeing our camping gear he cast even more aspersions on our genealogy and remarked on our presence on private land by telling us to depart forthwith (not his words). Realising that there was no point in explaining to a very cross man with a rifle, especially one we'd deprived of a kill, that we had permission to camp, we departed forthwith and tramped several weary miles in the dark back along the road to the bothy.

Brief encounter

Towards the end of the course the School gave us an indicator on our progress and the likelihood of passing our exams. We were given careers advice and information on various shipping companies that we should apply to for sponsored cadetships. One company I wrote to was B.I. (British India Steam Navigation Company). They seemed to like my application and asked me to their London HQ for an interview. I took a day train to London for an overnight stay before the interview. Back then trains still had a corridor and small compartments with sliding doors. The train wasn't busy from Aberdeen and by the time we stopped at Newcastle I was on my own. At Newcastle a middle-aged man came into the compartment to the seat opposite and we exchanged the normal pleasantries. Immediately I recognised his Shetland accent and he mine.

He said his name was Lowrie, so we chatted a bit about where I was going and Shetland news in general. It turned out that he was originally from Whalsay but now lived in the town of Corby, where he worked in a factory. The conversation turned to my native island of Yell, to which he remarked that there weren't many Frasers in Yell. I explained that my father was Walter Fraser and was originally from Burra Isle, so I wasn't exactly one of the Yell Frasers. This sparked considerable interest. He went on to say that he'd been shipmates with a Walter Fraser from Burra before the war. I replied that it was a small world, for my father was the only Walter Fraser from Burra I'd ever heard of, so it must have been my father on the ship with him. He replied that this couldn't be possible for I was too young and the Walter Fraser he'd known had been killed during the war. He'd heard that he'd been on an RFA oil tanker called the *British Lady* that had been lost with all hands. This was a bit of a mystery to me, but after he'd left the train at Peterborough I put it to the back of my mind as I had an interview to worry about.

My father, like most men that went through it, didn't talk about his wartime experiences unless directly asked about it. On my next trip home I mentioned my encounter with Lowrie on the train. To my surprise my father did know this Lowrie but he hadn't heard of him since they'd been shipmates. Yes, he'd sailed on an RFA tanker called the *British Lady,* and no they hadn't been sunk. They'd been attacked by a German bomber but the bomb had exploded alongside and hadn't caused too much damage. However, Lord Haw-Haw, in one of his pro-German propaganda broadcasts to Britain, had announced with some delight that the *British Lady* had been sunk with all hands. My father said that he'd gone home on leave after that voyage and walked into the house to find his parents in mourning for him. They too had been taken in by Lord Haw-Haw's broadcast.

Pride before a fail

Seamanship at the School was taught by Captain McKenzie, assisted by Jim the bosun who instructed us in ropework, knots and splices etc. One day, near the end of the course, while I was with the watch on board the *Robert Gordon*, Jim asked me to rig a bosun's chair so I could be hauled to the top of the main-mast, almost seventy feet above the deck, to do a job for him. This was no problem; even as far back as Mid Yell JS we'd practiced the knots for rigging a bosun's chair on a mast in the school play-shed. Getting a knot wrong could be lethal in rigging the chair for going aloft. Watched carefully by Jim, I rigged the chair and was hoisted up the mast, did the job and lowered myself down again. I met Jim a few years later on Union Street and we went for a beer and a chat. I reminded him of that day and asked him why he always picked Shetland lads for that kind of job. "You were the only ones that I could rely on not to tie a knot that would kill you!" was his reply.

Shortly before my trip to London our course results were announced and I was given top marks in the seamanship exam which included boat handling and man overboard recovery, ropework, signals etc. There was to be a prize-giving

Author (far right) on TS Robert Gordon; *1968.
Photo (c) Aberdeen Peoples Journal.*

a week before the end of the course and I was to be awarded the seamanship prize. Although I'd won school prizes at Mid Yell for essays and the like, this was the first achievement that I can say I was really proud of.

My interview with B.I. shore captains in their impressive London office must have gone well as I got a letter offering me a cadetship, conditional on passing a medical and the Board of Trade eyesight test. The BoT eyesight test was a mandatory test of distance and colour vision for all deck officers; failure meant you were unfit for service at sea. I hadn't given this much thought, as I'd been to the optician in Lerwick the previous year and he'd reported that my vision was okay, although one eye was slightly weaker than the other.

My eyesight test was conducted by the official BoT examiner in Aberdeen, who also would have done the tests for Mates' and Masters' Certificates. The colour chart test went with no problem at all. I was then marched into a darkened room where there was a lantern-slide projector and screen set up to simulate a vessel's navigation lights at night. After a few minutes to get accustomed to the gloom, pinpricks of lights in various combinations of red, green and white appeared and I had to call them out. This was repeated with one eye then with the other. At the end of the test he just said, "Your right eye does not meet the required standard of vision, therefore you are unfit for service at sea," then scribbled out a certificate to that effect. Right then and there my career as a deck officer in the Merchant Navy ended before it had even begun in earnest.

I did have a right to appeal the BoT examiner's decision by asking to have the test done by the BoT principal examiner in London. To do this I would need to be examined by an eye specialist to provide evidence to support my appeal. I went to an optician in Aberdeen as a first step. After an examination he suggested that I might scrape through another BoT test with my right eye but, in his opinion, it could well be worse when I returned for my Second Mate's examinations in two years time. That was it then. I had to decide if it was worth appealing and, if that was successful, worth the risk of failing the test later in my career. I wrote to B.I. explaining the situation and informed the School principal that I had failed the BoT test.

The following week was to be the School of Navigation prize-giving which was a public event hosting families and friends of the cadets. Top prizes for navigation (a sextant) and seamanship (binoculars) were donated by shipping lines that sent their representatives, usually retired senior captains, along to present them. The day after I'd told the School of my BoT test failure I was taken to one side by Captain McKenzie. On behalf of the School he informed me that I was not going to be presented with the seamanship prize as I wouldn't be going to sea due to the eye test failure. Apparently whoever was to present the prize always asked the recipient which shipping line he was joining. In my case this would be none, and for me to say so would be an embarrassment to the School of Navigation. I told him that I didn't feel like hanging around for the last two weeks anyway, so they could do what they wished (or words to that effect). I left that day, the only person who said goodbye and wished me luck was Jim the bosun, who I met at the gate as I left.

A change of course

I'd paid up my room at the Sailors Home for another week so I thought I'd spend the time trying to figure out my next move. Over the next few days I had a couple of chance meetings that required me to make a decision on which tack I should take regarding a future career. The morning after leaving the School I was idly throwing darts into the cafe dartboard when a lad sitting at the table asked if I wanted a game. It turned out that he was joining a ship as a radio officer, having qualified for his radio 'ticket' (P.M.G Certificate) at Aberdeen Technical College. A new course for a P.M.G. Certificate 2nd Class was due to start in a few weeks' time; this was a possibility that I had to consider. That same afternoon I made my way to Aberdeen Technical College and came back with information on the course. This wouldn't be the last time that a chance meeting would set me on a new tack in search of a career.

There must have been a nautical grapevine in operation for the day after I met the 'Sparks' a note was delivered to my room asking me to call along the Shipping Federation Office (colloquially, "the pool") just around the corner. Unbeknown to me the office was managed by an ex-merchant seaman from North Yell, now resident in Aberdeen, who'd heard of my predicament and asked me to drop in. At the pool office I met Basil, one of the kindest of men, who had been a good friend to many a Shetland sailor in the past. He offered to help me in any way he could. It turned out that he was also an agent for the New Zealand Shipping Company and gave me application forms to apply as an engineer apprentice. Now I had a second option to think about.

After asking around and finding out as much as I could about both seagoing options I felt that I needed to make a decision before heading home to Shetland. I knew nothing about electronics theory or practical, both a big part of the P.M.G. course, but I did know Morse code from the signals practical at the School of Navigation. I knew nothing about engineering or marine engines and I wasn't overly keen on spending much of my life, as I saw it, in the hot, confined spaces of an engine room. Better the one I knew a little bit about, so I applied for, and was accepted, on the Marine Radio Operators course.

Once back in Shetland I applied to the Shetland education authority for a bursary to see me through another year's accommodation in Aberdeen and buy course books. I explained the circumstances of my change of course and my reasons for needing a bursary. This was refused. Not only that, but they demanded the repayment of the bursary I'd been awarded for the deck officer's course; in their eyes I hadn't completed the course successfully! This was a problem. I had no money and I wasn't going to ask my parents to bail me out. Perhaps this was their careers officer getting back at me for the tree surgeon remark. Having nothing more to lose I asked for and got an appointment to see Shetland's Director of Education. He did agree to drop the repayment request, but only after I pointed out that the five O-levels and one Higher I gained in Aberdeen was better value for their money than a wasted year they had given me at Lerwick Central.

Although I knew that it would be difficult for them, I eventually agreed to let my parents fund me for the new course and I returned to Aberdeen. I found the course theory and some of the practical hard going but I was fine with getting up to Morse speeds required. I was still a couple of months short of my eighteenth birthday so all of the other students were a lot older than me, mostly with a background in electronics. I soon found that the course had started at a higher level of knowledge than I was at; ironically this was the same year that Yell became connected to mains electricity. When I got home for the Christmas break I could see that my parents were struggling with the winter croft work on top of extra knitting orders they were getting from the factory. I didn't say as much but I felt guilty about them having to fund my education on top of everything else.

I was worried that with another eight months of the course to go I might not pass at the end of it and that would be a big financial blow. I decided that I would drop out and spend the next eighteen months earning and saving enough funds to pay my way and start the course again when I was better prepared. I phoned the course director and although he tried his best to persuade me not to drop out he'd be happy for me to start again in the future. After Christmas 1968 I signed on the dole for the first and last time in my life.

Fit the Fifth: A Semester in the University of Life

Give a man a fish, and you feed him for a day. Teach a man to fish, and you feed him for a lifetime. (Often attributed to Maimonides.)

There were no jobs in Yell and nothing of interest in Lerwick (where I would need to find accommodation anyway). My plan was to help out at home during the rest of the winter and spring then see what was on offer by early summer. In March I had a reality check on life when I heard that Eric, who I'd become good friends with in Aberdeen, was one of the crew drowned in the Longhope lifeboat disaster. This was a hard shock that brought home a realisation that youth didn't equate to immortality. A nicer lad to have a beer and a game of darts with you couldn't wish to meet.

At Wasterhoose the 1969 lambing season came and went as did the 'voar' work and the peat cutting. With a possible return to the P.M.G. course still in mind, I was still looking for some employment, preferably to do with electronics and giving a decent wage. The 'Broo' had other ideas and I was offered work at Shetland Seafoods fish factory. The wage wasn't great but overtime could make up for that. The big attraction, however, was free sleeping accommodation in their fishworkers' huts beside Brown's Road, Lerwick. Joy!

'Wirkin' at da fish

I took the Overland to Lerwick the day before I was due to start work and signed on in Shetland Seafood's office from where I was allocated a bed in a hut and shown the factory canteen. The huts had dark green, painted, weatherboard cladding on the outside. Inside, a long corridor ran up the middle with four rooms on each side separated by hardboard partitions. The door on my room had long ago been replaced by a couple of blankets nailed to the door frame.

Each room had two beds supplied with a mattress and a couple of grey army blankets of dubious provenance; fortunately I'd brought my sleeping bag and a pillow with me. It turned out that my roommate was Magnus who'd been in my class at Mid Yell JS School. Last time I'd seen him had been the previous year in Aberdeen, where he'd run out of money and had slept on the floor of my room in the Sailors Home for a week.

Shetland Seafoods factory, Browns Road, Lerwick.
Accommodation hut entrance far right. Photo © Shetland Museum.

Two of the rooms had just had one occupant and were reserved for long term employees of Shetland Seafoods. One was Gibby, another Yell man, who worked on the fishmarket with Magnus. He'd been there for a number of years and had painted wonderful landscapes and seascapes on the interior hardboard panels of his room. In a single room at the far end of the hut lived old Geordie, who pretty much kept himself to himself. I think he had the night watchman's job at the factory. Sometimes he'd let us have hot kippers from the kiln if we'd rolled back from the pub in the late evening. I guess Geordie had his demons locked up in a bottle from which they would periodically escape. One evening as I was passing, his blanket door was pinned back and he called me in for a yarn. The grey, grizzled figure wearing a torn, brown, tweed jacket over a battered and stained blue boilersuit was sitting in a low chair. He was bent over a hissing primus stove on which a whole cod was being boiled in a 7lb jam tin. An open, half-consumed, half-bottle of whisky stood on the narrow window ledge by a crack in the grimy window pane. I can't remember now what we yarned about but he'd been a merchant seaman for many years. In total contrast to the ambiance of the hut, the room and the boiling fish was a bookshelf filling much of one wall. Geordie's reading included many classics of literature and poetry along with learned tomes on philosophy; just goes to show that you shouldn't judge a book by its cover.

The herring season hadn't started so I was allocated to a job in the whitefish part of the factory and would be working eight in the morning to five in the evening, Monday to Friday; Saturday's were overtime if required. The herring processing part of the factory would work Tuesday to Saturday. Each morning I'd clock in by punching my card in the machine by the factory door which recorded the time on the card. More than a minute late meant loss of fifteen minutes pay. Clocking in for somebody else who was late was a sackable offence.

My first job was standing at a conveyor belt along which fresh fish fillets from the filleters would pass; we'd pack these into large aluminium trays for freezing in the blast freezers. Each tray consisted of four compartments each holding about 7lb of fish fillets. My workmates on the packing belts were both male and female and varied from students on holiday jobs to Lerwick housewives. The job was repetitive and had to be done quickly and properly or one of the foremen (known as the "white coats") would have something to say. The job required long hours standing in the one spot with only the morning and afternoon tea-breaks and a lunch hour for relief. The otherwise mind-numbing boredom of the job was relieved by good natured banter across the belts (especially from the real housewives of Lerwick), but newcomers like myself soon learned to give as good as we got. After a couple of weeks I started getting a severe pain in my lower back from standing in one position by the belt. The lady next to me showed me a trick of varying my working height by standing on a fish-box for a time.

We got a lot busier when the herring season started. In those days much of the herring was still being caught sustainably by the traditional drift-netters, however, by now the much larger purse-netters and ring-netters had also joined the fleet. Compared to the drift-netters these were much more efficient and landed enormous catches of herring. To process the summer herring catch Shetland Seafoods employed students from all over the country (and some from Europe) as seasonal workers. These too were accommodated in the Brown's Road huts and in the old net store on Lerwick's Esplanade, known sometimes as the "Irish Hut" due to the large number of Irish students billeted there. This was a lively time as students came and went and the Irish Hut became the locus of many an entertaining evening.

Despite my best efforts my back pain would come on after an hour or so on the packing belt, but would disappear after moving round for a bit (still troubles me today if I stand in the same spot for too long). Harry, one of the white coats, noticed that I was periodically taking short walks away from the belt. When I explained he moved me onto another gang in the factory where I would have a lot more movement. This gang's job was drawing the trays of frozen fish fillets from the blast freezers, breaking out the frozen slabs onto a bench then packing them in cardboard cartons which we had to pre-assemble. These were closed when packed by wrapping wire straps around them in two directions, done on a machine, then loaded into a hoist running to the cold store on the floor above.

In the "Irish Hut"; 1969. Bill Law far left; Paul Murphy with guitar. Photo © Catherine Jamieson.

There were three of us in the gang: myself, Derek and Davy. One would break out the frozen slabs and send them down the rollers to the packer who would put four in each carton and send the carton along the rollers to the last in the line for wire strapping and feeding the hoist to the cold store. Breaking the slabs out of the frozen trays weighing over 28lbs was a fairly physically demanding job so we would take it in turns to do each job. One week near the end of my time there Davy was away and a Shetland guitar-playing legend took his place – Willie had been sent to join us by the 'Broo'. Although an entertaining workmate he wasn't just the most energetic member of the team so eventually Derek and I took it turn about on breaking out and carton strapping, leaving Willie on packing only. Another thing with Willie was that he often needed a break between official breaks, and he knew that we could arrange this "accidentally on purpose" by jamming the strapping machine. Sometimes when I was driving the machine Willie would look to see that there were no white coats around then give me his famous grin and whisper, "Ah'm needin a smok boy, jam da bugger."

During the winter I'd bought a second-hand Austin minivan with a view to getting lessons and passing my driving test to make myself more employable. When I started work in the factory I had it shipped to Lerwick and parked it outside the hut. Although I wasn't to know it at the time this was to lead to my very first, and memorable, experience as a tour guide. One Saturday morning I was giving the minivan a bit of a tidy up when two of my Irish student pals, Bill Law and Paul Murphy, along with a French girl came to see me. She was supposed to be catching a flight from Sumburgh that afternoon but there was no bus to the airport near her flight time; would I be willing to drive her to the airport along with her friends to see her off? I agreed, providing one of them had a full driving licence to comply with the law as I still hadn't passed my driving test. This caused a bit of hesitation and debate but Big Bill from Dublin declared that he had a full licence from Eire, would that do? I had no idea if that would cut any ice with the police if we were stopped but I was prepared to plead ignorance in my defence.

The French girl turned up at the appointed time with her rucksack and her friends, all five of them. As well as the French girl and myself, I had to fit into the small confines of a minivan no less than three big Irish lads, an Irish girl and an English girl. I then realised that getting all seven of us into the minivan was going to be a challenge; it only had two seats in the front and none in the back. Big Bill wasn't called that for nothing, being nearly as broad as he was tall and the other two lads weren't that small either. After some head scratching we dragged a mattress out of the hut to pad the back floor of the minivan and put two Irish lads and two girls in the back. Big Bill sat in the front passenger seat, the English girl squeezed in between us, unfortunately this left no room for me to change gear. The English girl said that she'd had driving lessons so the plan was that I would steer and she would change gear on my command. Funnily enough, we never thought that this arrangement might be even more illegal than not having a qualified driver. Our plan worked surprisingly well once we got clear of the town, although not the most comfortable drive I've ever made to Sumburgh.

Dem dry bones

After all our goodbyes had been said at the airport the rest of us decided to return via St Ninian's Isle that my Irish friends were keen to see. This is where, just eleven years earlier, a fabulous hoard of Pictish silver had been discovered buried beneath the floor of an early Christian chapel site. Above the early Christian chapel was the ruins of a 12th century chapel; this had been incorporated into a later graveyard that had been in use until the 19th century. All these layers of time had been exposed by the archaeological dig, but at that time there was no anti-rabbit fence to protect the site. When the archaeologists had stopped digging in the soft sandy soil the rabbits had not. With burials going back as far as pre-Christian times we could see that the rabbits had done a pretty good job of exhuming bones.

It turned out that the English girl was a medical student. As we walked across heavily-burrowed grass near the Chapel site she was, rather morbidly it seemed, identifying bones by exclaiming: "This is a bit of skull!" or "Finger bone!" or "Femur!" or "Mandible over here!" The rest of us found this exhibition of knowledge of the human skeleton a little unsettling, even more so when she produced a carrier bag and started collecting some of the larger examples. Although they said nothing, I could see that this was not going down well with the others. Eventually the Irish girl suggested leaving them reverently by the ruined chapel, but no, the reply was that these were just old bones from off the ground surface and taking a few for her university research was doing no harm.

After our visit we set off back to Lerwick in the minivan. Big Bill had been moved into the back to allow the tallest Irish lad to sit in the front as he was getting cramp. Back then the main road to Lerwick wasn't the straight fast road we have now, but winded its way uphill and down dale, still following the route of 19th century cart-tracks. I hadn't noticed that Big Bill was sitting on the back wheel arch, and as I negotiated a bend where the road dipped sharply I went into a pretty dramatic skid complete with a howling tyre squeal. Fortunately I regained control, just avoiding landing in the roadside ditch. It was a white knuckle ride for everybody, so I pulled over and stopped and we all got out checking that we hadn't got a puncture. We hadn't, it was just Bill's weight that had upset our balance on the corner. The Irish girl was clearly very upset, not with me, but screamed at the medical student whose fault she clearly thought it was. She then proceeded to give the unfortunate student, still clutching her bag of bones, a dressing down about removing bones from a Christian site. She refused to get back into the minivan if the bones were going to be in there with us. To resolve the situation I took her bag of dry bones and hid them beneath the small road-bridge over a burn saying that one day I would retrieve them and return them to St Ninian's Isle. Unfortunately road improvements beat me to it, so when much later I did have a chance to return them the little bridge was no longer there.

So long, and thanks for all the fish

With the August days getting noticeably shorter I got to thinking about job hunting again; as a seasonal worker I couldn't expect to be kept on beyond the middle of September. I wanted to stick to my plan of returning to the radio officer's course in a year's time, so with this in mind I began reading the job vacancies section in the local papers. The only advert that caught my eye was one by the Institute of Geological Sciences (IGS) for a Scientific Assistant at Lerwick Geophysical Observatory, about two miles outside Lerwick. I did some asking around and found out that this place was known as "da Wireless" on account of it having been a Royal Navy radio station during World War One. I also found out that the IGS shared the site with the Meteorological Office and had a hostel for accommodating their staff. I thought I'd nothing to lose by applying. Following my application I was invited to Edinburgh for an interview by the IGS. Shetland Seafoods kindly allowed me to take a few days off for this. The interview was a strange mix of asking what I knew about the Civil Service (if successful, I would be a civil servant) and about instruments, geology or geophysics, which amounted to very little. I wasn't offered the job. It was by an ironic twist of fate that many years later I was to obtain an honours degree in Earth Sciences, including geology and geophysics, and instigate Shetland's journey to become a Global Geopark.

Near the end of August most of the students were leaving and there was a sense of everything winding down. Jobs like washing out the fish-gut barrels with water hoses now became a chore rather than the opportunity for light-hearted banter and a chance to soak passers-by who gave cheek. One day the foreman came to me and asked if I would work in the cold store for a couple of weeks and then it would be time to collect my P45 and my final pay packet. Cold store work was an interesting diversion from the other jobs I'd done in the factory, but was tempered with the knowledge that I would be unemployed in the very near future.

On the Friday evening after I picked up my penultimate pay packet I bought the local paper and stopped by the Thule bar for a beer while I scanned the job page. The Thule was a bar I rarely frequented, but that evening it was just a handy place to read the paper. With nothing promising in the paper I was finishing my beer and was about to leave when in walked George, a classmate from Lerwick Central School. I hadn't seen him since those days, so we had a bit of catching up to do. It turned out that he'd joined the Meteorological Office shortly after leaving school and now worked at Lerwick Observatory. He'd heard of my failed application to join the IGS and suggested that I try the Met Office, as they were also looking for staff. Next week I said goodbye to my workmates at Shetland Seafoods and so ended an experience of a lifetime.

Shetland Seafood's factory and the huts are no longer there; the Mareel cinema and arts centre now stands on the site of the lower factory. The site where we washed out the barrels that held stinking fish guts is now the location of the infamous "White House" offices of Shetland Islands Council. Some may form an opinion on the appropriateness of this choice of site but, like Urquhart in *House of Cards*, I couldn't possibly comment.

Full circle

With no proper jobs on offer, and the door of the dole office looming large, I took George's advice and applied to join the Met Office. I then had an interview with the superintendent at Lerwick Observatory. My application was accepted, with a proposed start date of 1st October 1969. I had now joined the Civil Service as a Ministry of Defence civilian working for the Meteorological Office as a Trainee Scientific Assistant. I had a couple of weeks home before I was due to start. In true Civil Service manner, instead of filling the vacancy at Lerwick Observatory, I found myself posted to the Met Office at RAF Kinloss on the Moray Firth as an airfield weather observer. I can only assume the rationale behind this was that someone had looked for Shetland on the map and seen the islands' inset box in the Moray Firth and posted me accordingly. On the RAF base I was billeted in the Sergeant's Mess (apparently I now had the civilian equivalent rank of a Flight Sergeant!). My first day at work I was given a notepad, a copy of the International Cloud Atlas, and told to get on with it. "This'll do me 'til I find a proper job," I thought.

Thirty-four years later I was still in the employ of the Met Office and still looking for a proper job. I'd worked in Kinloss, London, East Anglia, Ocean Weather Ships, Lerwick (twice), Sumburgh Airport, Reading, Belfast International

Airport, Glasgow and finally at Port Control, Sella Ness for the Port of Sullom Voe, Shetland; in that time I'd worked in various disciplines, climbing to the (not so dizzy) heights of Higher Scientific Officer weather forecaster.

Ocean Weather Ship Weather Reporter.

Met Office crew on OWS Weather Reporter; 1974
Left to right: Bill Flanders; Paddy Jennings; Allen Fraser;
Vince Dunphy; Geoff Allen; Derek Ogle; Adrian Henley.

My last ten years working for the Met Office was at Sella Ness. I was now forecasting and advising harbour pilots on weather for the handling of supertankers at Europe's largest oil terminal at Sullom Voe. Two of these harbour pilots had been on my course at the School of Navigation back when this all started. A wheel had turned full circle. When the Met Office contract with the Port ended I took an early retirement package. With no immediate plans I was waiting for fate to take a hand again.

Phase Two

**The Guide is definite.
Reality is frequently inaccurate.**
(Douglas Adams)

Fit the Sixth: On the Rocks

Sometimes I tink whin da Loard med da 'aert',
An He got it aa pitten tagidder,
'Fan' He still hed a 'nev-foo' a 'clippins' left ower,
Trimmed aff o dis place or da 'tidder',
An He hedna da hert ta 'baal' dem awa,
For dey lookit dat boannie an rare,
Sae He fashioned da Isles fae da ends o da aert,
An med aa-body fin at hame dere.
(A verse from *Shetlandic* by Rhoda Bulter.)

Geologically speaking, Shetland is indeed put together from small slices of the same rock formations that make up Scotland, Western Norway and Eastern Greenland. Shetland's geological history goes back almost three billion years and the "nev-foo a clippins" has been slowly brought together over all that time by Earth's tectonic forces. Shetland's unique landscape, natural history, history and culture are all due to that long geological journey as I discovered by chance meetings and a fatal accident.

Over the Moon

I'd been in the employ of the Met Office for nearly ten years, since I'd left the fish factory, so was in a bit of a rut and ready for a new challenge. One clear, moonlit evening I was returning home when I saw my neighbour in his garden pointing a long stick at the Moon. After exchanging remarks about werewolves, green cheese and jumping cows, he said that he was measuring the diameter of the Moon. A statement I initially thought was in the same category of banter. It turned out that he was indeed using a measured stick with a disk attached (to cover the Moon) to calculate the Moon's diameter. He explained that he'd just started an Open University Science Foundation Course, hence the Moon experiment. A couple of beers later he'd convinced me that maybe this was a course of study that I could have a go at.

I started my OU degree course in 1980 at foundation level. My plan over the next few years was to gain my degree by studying mainly mathematics and physics, mainly to keep my employer happy since they'd agreed to pay for my courses. Three years later, to fill a space in my academic programme, I took a geology course. I found geology much more interesting than the calculus course that I was studying the same year. Both courses had summer schools at Durham University. The calculus summer school was notable only for having the same tutor as the child prodigy Ruth Lawrence, who, aged ten, became the youngest person ever to win a place at Oxford. The geology summer school was much more interesting. This required a lot of field work in the outdoors which easily worked up a thirst for the student's bar in the evening. One evening a couple came into the bar with a handful of forms seeking new members to join the Open University Geological Society; for the price of a pint I was hooked. I signed on the dotted line, a decision that in the long term proved to be a life changing one. My studies changed direction from then on. I took courses mainly in geological disciplines, and eventually I obtained a BSc (Hons) in Earth Sciences.

A tour guide is born

My geology studies opened my eyes for the first time to an understanding of Shetland's rocks and our spectacularly diverse landscape. At school we'd been told little or nothing about Shetland's unique natural history and even less about our human history and our culture that sprang from it. Shetland's geology is both complex and exciting with an extensive variety of rock types and geological processes packed into a geographically small island group. The only books available on Shetland geology were one on the geology of Orkney and Shetland and another on the geology of Western Shetland, both by Edinburgh geologist Wally Mykura. These were both a bit dated and written for professional geologists in an old-school academic style that was a struggle for students and amateurs like myself to get their heads around.

To my delight the Open University Geological Society that I'd joined in Durham decided to make its first ever visit to Shetland in 1987. This was to be a week-long geology field excursion led by Wally Mykura and I was asked to organise the transport for the group since I was working in Shetland. I liaised with the trip organiser and all went well – travel, accommodation and transport were all booked – until just about a week before the start date. I got a call one morning saying that there had been a tragic road accident in Edinburgh and Wally Mykura had been killed. The group and Wally's relatives had agreed that because everyone's travel to Shetland had been booked, the trip should still go ahead. I was then asked if I'd be prepared to lead it using the itinerary prepared by Wally. I'd never been on a week-long geology trip before, never mind lead one and I certainly didn't have the geological knowledge to stand in front of a rock outcrop and lecture a group. I did, however, know where all the localities on the itinerary were. In the end I did the navigation and another geologist came from Edinburgh to do the explanations. The trip went well, the weather was kind and everyone went home happy. It was a life changing week.

The experience of having Shetland's geology and landscape explained from the rock face enthused me to go on other field excursions elsewhere in Britain and abroad as I studied for my degree. The more I did this I came to realise that Shetland could match anywhere for a large variety of classic geological exposures, all easily accessible within a small geographical area. On one Scottish trip we'd driven for two hours then hiked across boggy moors in pouring rain to view Hutton's classic outcrop of granite in a river bed. I could have visited a better example just five minutes walk from a Shetland roadside wearing carpet slippers, but unfortunately James Hutton, "Father of Modern Geology", never came to Shetland. Shetland has the distinct advantage of allowing easy access to the same variety of geology in a day that it would take most of a week to visit in mainland Scotland.

Professor Derek Flinn of Liverpool University had spent a professional lifetime working on Shetland geology so I amassed a collection of his published papers to study. Over time I was able to research and design my own geological excursion itineraries in Shetland. Although I was still working for the Met Office I was asked to lead occasional Shetland geology trips for the OUGS and other geological societies. Just by chance I'd become a geology tour guide, albeit a hobby one.

Geology group examine folded rocks in the Burn of Kirkhouse, Voe.

Geopark Shetland

A couple of years before I took early retirement Ann, my wife, and me had been on a trip to the northern part of the Greek island of Lesvos. Northern Lesvos was much quieter and economically worse off than the touristy south. In order to attract more visitors to the north, an area of their petrified forest had been developed into a tourist attraction with an interpretation trail through the stone trees. A small museum and visitor centre had been built to explain the geology of the forest; in addition it sold crafts and produce from the local area. Lesvos Geopark was one of the first European Geoparks in the Geopark movement. The purpose of the Geoparks Network is to boost local economies through tourism and education by the promotion and interpretation of world class geology of an area. Another Geopark we visited was the Marble Arch Caves in County Fermanagh which was working hard in developing tourist facilities in their area.

About the time I left the Met Office I wrote an article in *The Shetland Times* lauding the European Geoparks Network. In it I suggested that although Shetland's geology and associated landscapes was undoubtedly world class, we were a geological backwater, ignored by geology students and tourists alike. I pointed out that Shetland's amazing geodiversity offered great potential as a teaching area for classic geology. Our wonderful landscape and culture came from our geology, yet we had a tourism industry that promoted Shetland almost exclusively in terms of Shetland ponies and puffins. I suggested that Shetland would be an ideal candidate to join the European Geoparks Network. There I thought it would end, but I was wrong. Following my article I was asked to make a presentation on Geoparks to Shetland's local government development agencies and Shetland Amenity Trust, the organisation that looks after our culture and heritage.

Following my presentation, I was given a three-month contract to find out what Shetland needed to do to have a European Geopark. To tell Shetland's story properly I recommended that the whole of Shetland become a Geopark and with that in mind I drafted our application document to the European Geoparks Network. This I did with advice and help from established Geoparks in Ireland and Wales. There was some immediate opposition to the concept in Shetland from those who viewed anything with the suffix "park" with deep suspicion, equating it, quite wrongly, with additional rules and restrictions. In fact the Geopark ethos is to work wholly within the existing legislation of a parent country without the need for any new rules, regulations or restrictions.

A Geopark Shetland working group was set up and a full-time geology project officer employed to take our application forward. After a lot of hard work by successive geology project officers putting interpretations in place and opening geological trails, Geopark Shetland was designated a Global and European Geopark in 2009. In 2015 the United Nations Educational, Scientific and Cultural Organisation (UNESCO) awarded Geopark Shetland formal recognition. UNESCO Geopark status is to geology and landscape what their World Heritage

A TOWN CALLED TOILETS

Status is to archaeology and architecture. Our UNESCO accreditation was a well-deserved testament to years of hard work and dedication by Robina Barton, Geopark Shetland's geology project officer, in promoting our region, putting on educational activities and writing interpretations.

*Geopark Shetland Geowall at Mavis Grind.
A cross-sectional model of the rocks across Northmaven.*

Geologists examine sediments and lava flows at Aesha Head, Papa Stour.

Shetland Geotours

Following my three-month Geopark contract I had no plans. At one of our Geopark working group meetings I had been asked about geological tours. Although I still led the odd week-long field trip for geology groups every couple of years or so, I didn't do it as a business. It was suggested by one of the economic development officers that I should think about setting up a tour-guiding business offering daily tours for visitors to Shetland.

Running my own business was something that had never even crossed my mind, far less a tour-guiding one. I soon realised that geology-specific tours alone wouldn't pay its way. In order to appeal to a wider spectrum of tourists I would need to follow the Geopark ethos and combine Shetland's geology and landscape with its history and culture. I spent about a year working out a daily schedule of tour routes and details. I knew our geology and landscape and, having grown up in Shetland, I was familiar with the flora and fauna. I'd experienced Shetland's crofting and fishing history at first hand but I wasn't so sure about our archaeology or the social history of individual parts of Shetland, so I did a lot of research on this. I commissioned a website to advertise my tours on the internet and take bookings by email. I signed up with the Lerwick Tourist Centre, run by Visit Scotland, to take bookings on my behalf. My biggest challenge was to purchase a suitable vehicle for taking my guests on tour; in this I was lucky to have a vehicle sourced for me on the Scottish Mainland. I purchased a two-year-old, nine-seat Ford Tourneo Transit minibus and by the summer of 2005 I was all ready to go.

The author with Shetland Geotours minibus.

It took over two years for the business to get established. I was grateful for help and friendly advice I received from Elma Johnson who ran Island Trails, a great ambassador for Shetland and a tireless promoter of all that is great about Shetland. Sadly Elma passed away just a few years later. Indeed all the other tour-guiding businesses were helpful and we cooperated with each other rather than competed. All the heritage centres and cafes that I included in my tour itineraries always gave a first-class welcome to my guests and this made my job so much easier. I was lucky enough to secure a contract with a travel company, Wildabout Orkney, who sent their clients to Shetland and I had a great working relationship with them.

Over one third of my bookings came from walk-ins to the Visit Scotland Tourist Centre in Lerwick. The excellent front desk staff at the Tourist Centre were amazingly helpful all through my tour-guiding career and it would have been almost impossible to run a business without them. The Centre itself was poorly managed for the first few years and introduced impractical gimmicks and rules that made the booking process for potential customers extremely difficult. Fortunately the appointment of new management brought a much needed improvement to bookings.

Being my own boss and running my own business was a fantastic challenge. I enjoyed the experience for eleven years until wear and tear on the minibus was becoming apparent. I guess wear and tear on the owner was probably also becoming apparent now that I was officially an old age pensioner! Purchase costs of a new vehicle would require another ten years of fully committing my summers to tour guiding. Since there were other things that I'd wanted to do before shuffling off this mortal coil, I decided to quit while I was ahead. I loved tour guiding and meeting such a wide spectrum of people from all over the world. In the following chapters I recount some of the characters I met and some of the experiences we shared.

Fit the Seventh: Sights, Sites and Sightings

It's not what you look at that matters, it's what you see.
(Henry David Thoreau, American essayist and practical philosopher.)

Many visitors arriving in Shetland express surprise that the islands of Shetland and Orkney are visually so very different; evidence perhaps of a failure by the tourism industry to promote Shetland in the way they should. Not everyone can appreciate the beauty and value of the diverse Shetland landscape we are so very fortunate to live in. Sadly there are those who don't wish for anyone to appreciate and enjoy Shetland as they see no value in scenery. Some of the worst offenders in this are native Shetlanders. One farmer I met asked what my minibus (with Shetland Geotours writ large on the sides) was for and what was I doing. When I explained, he said, "I dunna ken why you wid want ta bring folk tae Shetland, there's damn all here for dem tae see!"

Unfortunately, this is precisely the attitude expressed by those who intend to cover Shetland's hills with hundreds of giant, industrial-sized wind turbines and associated infrastructures. The ongoing development of industrial wind farms will ravage our moorland and carve up our hills with hundreds of kilometres of wide access roads and dozens of huge quarries. It is depressing to think that the pleasant rolling hills and upland valleys we see today, due to Shetland missing the worst effects of the last glaciation, is now to be despoiled by windfarm developers. Egged on by our national and local politicians, those behind this mindless exploitation of our landscape have shown no consideration as to the destructive effects on the environment, scenery and people of the vast and permanent industrial footprints of their windfarms. Shetland's unique landscape will be changed forever.

Scenic inland moorland valley and hills soon to be destroyed by industrial windfarm development.

Visitors' vistas

I have never met a visitor who wasn't impressed by Shetland's unique mixture of landscapes and seascapes. One quote I remember from a guest when we were halfway through a tour: "There's just a WOW around every corner, isn't there?"

Another was by a hard-case American oilman from a drilling vessel berthed in Lerwick. I took him on a tour of North Mainland and the cliffs of Esha Ness. When we got back I asked him what he thought of Shetland.

He replied, "Gotta be in my top three places I've been."

So I asked what the other two were.

"Grand Canyon and Mount McKinley Range in Alaska."

The number of potential viewpoints and photo-stops on any tour through Shetland is almost limitless. As well as making request stops I used a number of favoured stopping points. At some of those we'd take a short walk. One of the stops was at Mavis Grind where the Atlantic and the North Sea are separated by a narrow neck of land between high hills. Before reaching this stop I would often tell my guests to prepare to do the coast to coast walk from the North Sea to the Atlantic. Some would look worried at the prospect of a long hike until they came to see that the distance between coasts is a mere eighty metres. Guiding a couple of ladies, I'd arrived there on a day when the cloud overhead had Sullom Voe (North Sea side) in a grey shadow while the Atlantic side was below a clear blue sky. One lady asked how you can tell the difference between the North Sea and the Atlantic. I pointed to both sides and jokingly remarked that the North Sea was grey and the Atlantic bright blue. She took my explanation literally, thinking the difference between the two to be permanent; a lesson to me to be careful about off-the-cuff remarks, but one I sometimes forgot.

*Mavis Grind from coast to coast. North Sea
in the left, Atlantic Ocean on the right.*

Some of my tours were for those who wanted longer walks. Walking the Volcano Trail along the sheer cliffs composed of lava and ash of Esha Ness was the most popular. I also guided walks to the Iron Age broch at Cullswick as part of a moorland and cliff walk. The walk from Burrafirth to Hermaness across the National Nature Reserve in Unst was a popular walk ending with superb views across Muckle Flugga to Outstack, the full stop at the top of Britain. When requested, I occasionally guided an even longer walk around the spectacular island of Papa Stour. Guided walks show some of the best scenery Shetland has to offer, especially if there are encounters with wildlife such as seals, otters, mountain hares and the shy 'whitrit'. Birdlife on moorland, loch, sea and cliff are highlights on any tour, including the destructive, winged vermin of the skies - the bonxie (Great Skua). Unfortunately the bonxie is now promoted in some quarters as a major tourist attraction to Shetland; being attacked by a bonxie is now regarded by some as a "must have" experience. In reality, the uncontrolled population explosion of this bird has caused it to become a predator to many rare moorland birds as well as seabirds such as the kittiwake, which it has wiped out on some islands.

Some tour operators run wildlife specific tours for photographers. Driving my own tour one day along a single track road I came upon another minibus stopped in the middle of the road ahead. Suddenly windows and sliding doors

On Herma Ness with a walking group.

opened on one side and about a dozen huge long camera lenses poked out almost simultaneously. One of my guests remarked, "Looks just like cannon being run out at the battle of Trafalgar!"

There are many remarkable vistas to be found in Shetland, no two landscape or seascape views are the same. These change with the season, with the weather and with the time of day as the light changes. Truly our islands are a dream location for the photographer or the artist. One year I had the pleasure of the company of two quite elderly, retired art teachers on several of my tours. We stopped at all the usual viewpoints, and while my other guests messed about with their cameras, these two ladies brought out sketch pads and a small tray of watercolour paints and brushes. It was an education to watch them capture the essence of every viewpoint with just a few brushstrokes just as quickly as the photographers with their cameras.

A professional photographer from the USA gave me my longest day ever of tour guiding. I'd met him in the Tourist Centre and he asked me if I could take him to as many scenic spots as I could the next day as it was his only full day in Shetland. I agreed and enquired at what time he'd like to be collected from his hotel.

"What time is sunrise?" he asked.

"About 5am," I replied.

"Come and get me about 4am then. I wanna catch the sunrise; you take me to a good spot."

I collected him at four in the morning and he got a good sunrise over the Isles of Gletness. We covered the whole East and North Mainland during the day and evening. He took his last photo at 10pm on the Braewick beach, Eshaness. For that tour I'd left home at 3.40am and got back at 11pm.

Weather

As a guide I often had to dispel urban myths about Shetland. No, our lack of tree cover is not because Shetland is too windy for them to grow; it's because trees can't grow on the deep peat blanket that covers our hills and we don't plant forests on our green agricultural land. No, Shetland isn't the windiest place in Britain. We aren't the wettest place either; for example, we get less than half the rainfall experienced in the West Highlands of Scotland. In fact our spring and summers can be very dry, and we don't have the same midge problem found in the West of Scotland. We don't have hot summers or snowy winters because we are a small landmass regulated by the temperature of the Atlantic which keeps us cool in summer and mild in winter. Our weather can be highly variable at times, so it is true to say that visitors should come prepared to experience all four seasons in an afternoon.

Esha Ness volcanic cliffs wear their summer coat.

Esha Ness cliffs after a winter storm.

Even the odd spell of poor weather can't detract from the Shetland experience, only enhance it in a different way. That is until someone loses something and panic to find it sets in. On one geology group trip a lady said she'd lost her geological hammer, so I asked her where she had it last. She concluded she'd left it by a rock outcrop about half a mile away. We hiked back there in pouring rain, searched around and couldn't find it anywhere, then hiked back to the minibus again. When we got back she found it beneath her seat. A few years later I'd walked with a group to Hermaness but heavy rain and hill fog had caught us on the way back. Everyone had waterproofs to put on so that was okay. When we got back to the minibus and disrobed again a Swiss girl announced she'd dropped her camera with all her holiday photos somewhere on the way back. Could she (meaning we) go back and look for it? Remembering the hammer episode I suggested she check all her pockets and underneath her seat before we did anything else. Sure enough there it was, it had fallen on the floor of the minibus out of her waterproof pocket.

My weather forecasting skills were often useful for planning tour itineraries, especially if longish walks were involved. Summer fog could be a vexation, however if there was a 'steekit-stumnaa' on one side of Shetland, visibility on the other side would usually be relatively clear. Only twice in eleven years was the fog so all enveloping of the islands that I cancelled tours; taking money from my clients to sit and listen to a view was something my conscience wouldn't allow. There was one occasion when a small group had booked for a guided walk along the Esha Ness cliffs. On the appointed day sea-fog had filled St Magnus Bay and lay in a thick blanket across Esha Ness. I informed the group that there was little or no prospect of the fog clearing and they'd just be wasting their money. However they insisted that they wanted to try the walk anyway, so I drove them to the Esha Ness lighthouse and we set off for a walk along the cliff tops. The fog was so thick that the sea at the bottom couldn't be seen from the top of the cliffs. The sun would occasionally try to shine down on us through the fog thus casting weird shadows and turning the fog from grey to white. As we walked the swirling white fog around the dark volcanic headlands caused them to appear then fade like mystifying apparitions. Silhouettes of eroded cliff edges against the fog often took on the appearance of contorted faces. The absolute stillness of our uncanny cliff top world created an eerie atmosphere that magnified the sound of invisible waves booming from the impenetrable voids below. My guests and I agreed that it was a walk well worth doing just to experience Esha Ness in a different light.

A weather-dependent tour I offered each Sunday during the season was to the island of Mousa. Mousa provided the ideal combination of a boat trip followed by not too long a walk where we would encounter land and sea birds as well as seals. There are some nice geological outcrops along the walk that provide evidence of a time when Mousa's rocks were forming in a hot desert valley. Walls and buildings along the way tell of the island's last human occupants. Earlier inhabitants in the Iron Age built a broch which is now the best preserved of its kind, but is an archaeological enigma that begs more questions than provides answers. As a guide I would take my clients at a fairly slow pace around the trail on the island as in good weather there is plenty of time to stop, look and explain. Others, arriving off the boat without a guide tend to hurry on ahead and often miss out on a lot.

Sometimes the weather would change quite quickly and catch those not dressed properly unawares. This happened on a trip into Mousa with an Iranian gentleman and a young French couple. The morning was dry but with a cool easterly breeze. As rain was forecast for later I had advised the group to bring waterproofs just in case. The rain arrived early, just as we were landing on the island. It was accompanied by a raw east wind that meant we'd be quite exposed on the walk around much of the island trail. Even so, all three were keen to do the walk as they'd come prepared with waterproofs. It was at this point that the Iranian gentleman mentioned that he'd had a triple heart bypass operation just six weeks before, but he thought he'd be all right if we didn't walk too fast. Although the walk is only just over two kilometres in distance, this wasn't a risk I felt it sensible to let him take given the weather, but I was going to have to be a bit tactful.

I also noticed that although the French couple had waterproof coats, they wore shoes more suited for Avenue des Champs Elysées than the mires of Mousa. I had a quiet word with the boat skipper and we agreed that in view of the weather I could tell my guests that the boat would need to return early so we would only have time to walk the sheltered short route to the broch and back. That way they all got to visit the broch without too much risk to life and limb. The rain became quite heavy and the coats of the French couple had the characteristic of directing the runoff straight into their chic suburban footwear. The next day, before taking another tour with me, I had to direct them to the Lerwick shops to replace their fashionable footwear that had completely disintegrated while drying out on hotel radiators.

Safety first

Safety of my guests was always my first concern, but personal safety had to be their own responsibility. Although I would never take anyone to somewhere that was dangerous, I had to be aware that for some the great outdoors was an unfamiliar environment where I couldn't rely on the normal rules of common sense to apply. This was ably demonstrated on one Mousa trip when we caught up with a young Italian couple photographing a line of 'peerie-scarfs' drying their wings close by the foot of a twenty metre high cliff. Nothing unusual in this except that the lad, laden with camera equipment, had walked out onto a narrow finger of rock that jutted out from the top of the sheer drop. What he hadn't realised, and his watching wife hadn't noticed, that there was a large zigzag crack right through the rock finger. The only thing holding him from a plunge to eternity was just a few centimetres thickness of weathered sandstone. As he was standing right on the point of the rock finger with the camera to his eye, and not wanting to alarm him, I tapped his wife on the shoulder and pointed to the very obvious zigzag crack. I expected his wife to quietly ask him to get back to safety, but no, she just screamed at him. I thought for an awful second he would jump right off the cliff, but fortunately he didn't and made a quick retreat to safety.

Rock finger on Mousa that a photographer thought would make a good perch.

Another heart-stopping moment came by way of a mother and daughter from California. The mother was originally from Aberdeen but had gone to live in California when she was fourteen years old. Even after thirty-odd years living there she had retained her Aberdonian accent. The daughter worked for a Californian law firm and was very much a city person but extremely excited by the whole Shetland experience. On a sunny summer's day, with Shetland's West Mainland looking at its best, I'd walked with them from Culswick out to the broch then south along the high cliffs opposite the Burga Stacks. From this high point there is a stunning view inland across to a headland called the Nev. We'd walked down the slope just a short distance from the high point when the daughter produced her small camera. "Gee, can I get a photo of you and Mom together, with that view behind you?"

Mom and I turned to face her as she raised her camera. To get the whole scene in her viewfinder she started running backwards up the slope. For a split second I thought she must know what she's doing, then I shouted, "STOP!"

"What is it?" she said, rather crossly, stopping and lowering her camera.

"Look behind you."

She did. She was standing about two metres from a sixty-metre drop to the sea below. We were all quite shaken. She apologised to me and Mom saying that

The Nev, Culswick, West Mainland.

she was just so taken in by the view that she completely forgot she was near a cliff top.

Ever after that incident, if I thought someone was going to do it, I would warn them not to walk while holding cameras or binoculars to their eyes. Sometimes I felt that I needed eyes in the back of my head as the only serious accidents happened to those who wandered off to do their own thing. One lady, an experienced outdoor person and botanist, wandered off among the granite boulders on the top of Collafirth Hill and slipped and dislocated the middle finger of her left hand. She casually walked back to the rest of the group and held out her hand and asked me if I would mind putting it back in. It was dislocated so much that it was almost at right-angles to the ring finger. No way was I going to attempt that. I made a sling to hold her hand against her chest and drove her back to Accident and Emergency in Lerwick.

Another camera and footwear incident happened when I was guiding a large group of professional and hobby geologists from the London-based Geologists' Association for week of field excursions. It was a group of over twenty so I engaged the help of Laura, a geology student, to act as the eyes in the back of my head. I was usually at the head of the group and Laura's job was to be at the back to make sure nothing got left behind and everyone was accounted for. There was one chap who took a lot of photos at each locality we visited and was always last to leave, so Laura would wait for him to catch up with the group. I'd been examining the lava flows beneath the Esha Ness cliffs at Breigeo with the group then we moved back up to the cliff top leaving the photographer and Laura to catch up when he'd finished. We'd just reached the top when Laura called out, "He's fallen!" Not the words I wanted to hear in the vicinity of thirty metre high cliffs.

I instructed the rest of the group to stay where they were while I and another trained first aider from the group went back down the cliff to see what had happened. The gentleman in question was sitting on a rock with his leg stretched out saying that he'd turned his ankle. We could immediately see from the acute angle his foot made with his leg that this was going to be much, much worse than a simple sprain. We checked that he wasn't bleeding so there was little else we could do other than make him comfortable. The next problem was to get him out of there and to hospital. I called the coastguard who sent the local volunteer cliff rescue team. Within forty minutes of my call they'd assembled on our remote cliff top location with Land Rover, winch, shear-legs and stretcher. They did a very professional job of getting him on a stretcher and winching him up to the cliff top. From there we carried him on the stretcher for about a kilometre to the nearest road where the ambulance and paramedics were waiting.

In hospital they found that his ankle had been dislocated and broken in three places. Laura told me afterwards that he'd been walking across the lava flow while editing and deleting images on his camera and had gone over on his ankle by stepping on a small ridge in the rock. He was wearing trainers with thick soles but no ankle support, hence the severe damage resulting in months in plaster. On a slightly lighter note, only a BP geologist and I in the group had first responder first aid training. There were also three professors of medicine in the group, but thankfully their skills were not required on this occasion. One was a professor of haematology (he wasn't bleeding), the other two were pathologists (he was still alive).

Lava flows at Brei Geo, Esha Ness. Where a photographer broke his ankle and had to be winched up the cliff.

Centres of attraction

Apart from the magnificent Shetland Museum in Lerwick, Shetland has fourteen Heritage Centres or museums; all are different and reflect the many facets of Shetland's unique natural history, human history and culture. Thankfully none have gone down the road of electronic touch screens with their dumbed down text and sweeping generalisations. Heritage Centres are staffed by enthusiastic members of the local community and were a big hit with my guests who were always very complimentary about their visits to them. It would be difficult to compare the popularity of one Heritage Centre with another, each has a different characteristic. All have real artefacts on show and staff who know about their history. For example the Crofthouse Museum, a restored Shetland croft house from the 1850s, has a dialect speaking, present-day crofter as one of its curators. I have great difficulty convincing some of my guests that the Crofthouse isn't his real home; he doesn't actually live in it.

Crofthouse Museum, South Voe, Boddam.

All these centres and their staff are a great asset to Shetland's tourism industry and to native Shetlanders, yet many tourists and locals who would enjoy a visit don't know that they exist. This is due to the failure of the tourism industry to adequately publicise them; leaflets on a few stands is just not enough. In addition there are many more unmanned geological sites and archaeological sites, some of which have interpretive panels. Unfortunately many of these sites also don't get the promotion or recognition by our tourist industry they deserve, some sites are sadly neglected by those tasked with looking after them.

The visitor to Shetland will also find several magnificent gardens that are open to visitors. Rosa and James's Lea Gardens in Tresta, Michael's Wood in Eid and Da Gairdins in Sand are all living proof that Shetland is not the windswept wilderness some imagine it to be. The archaeological sites of Jarlshof and Old Scatness, both close to Sumburgh airport, always drew favourable comments from my guests. Jarlshof presents a wonderful four-thousand-year-long timeline of well preserved buildings from the Neolithic through the Bronze Age, Iron Age, Pictish and Viking times to Norse Medieval and Scots 16th century. Many of my guests rated Jarlshof higher than Skara Brae World Heritage Site on Orkney. Jarlshof has portable audio guides for visitors to use as they walk around the site, but I preferred to guide my guests myself as I'd put a lot of time and effort into studying the history and layout of the site.

Old Scatness is an extraordinarily well preserved Iron Age broch and village; it was once regarded as one of the premier archaeological sites in Europe. When I started my tour-guiding business Old Scatness was a vibrant place, open six days a week with several excellent onsite guides taking visitors through the excavated broch and houses. Also on site were living history demonstrators using local stone and other materials in reconstructed Iron Age and Pictish houses. In the small visitor centre there were demonstrations of weaving and other craft skills from our history; children could dress up and play a Viking game. It was a vibrant place with something for everyone. When I was preparing Shetland's Geopark application I used the Old Scatness experience as an example of how our aspiring Geopark was bringing together geology, archaeology, history and culture all on one site. Here I could show that not only was Old Scatness a popular tourism attraction, it was also a big draw for Shetland residents who were fascinated to find out how their distant ancestors lived and worked.

All the onsite guides and demonstrators were excellent, but one in particular wowed my guests with her clear and well thought-out explanations. No matter what the weather threw at her, or how many times she'd guided a tour each day, her infectious enthusiasm never waned as she brought the dwellers of our Iron Age past to life. After visiting Old Scatness an Australian guest was so impressed by Jane's guiding skills he remarked to me that he would give her a job any day. So I asked if he employed guides in Australia.

"Yes," he said. "We employ all the guides for Sydney Opera House, and that girl is the best I've ever heard."

Unfortunately the importance and potential of Old Scatness was never appreciated by our local government, our tourism industry, or those charged with looking after our heritage. Over the years it was starved of the investment, planning and publicity it needed so declined into a poor shadow of its former self. At its best Old Scatness was a tourism jewel in Shetland's crown, rated by my visitors as being an even better experience than Jarlshof. Sadly I had to

*Site guide Jane enthrals a group in an
Iron Age roundhouse at Old Scatness; 2006.*

drop it from my tour itinerary as due to neglect and decline it had become an embarrassment and could only partially open one day per week. I found it difficult to explain to visitors why some of our important sites are neglected while others are well maintained. For example, the remote Neolithic site of Stanydale Temple in West Mainland gets comparatively few visitors compared to the early Christian Chapel on the iconic St Ninian's Isle. Stanydale is well maintained with grass trimmed weekly, while the Chapel, one of only four of its kind in Shetland and with a nationally important Christian history, remains neglected and overgrown with thistles and nettles.

*St Ninian's Isle. The sand tombolo is built up by Atlantic swell
waves being diverted evenly around both sides of the island.*

St Ninian's Isle Chapel and graveyard. This historically important site is left unmarked and overgrown.

The importance of St Ninian's Isle Chapel in the story of bringing Christianity to Shetland is overshadowed by the discovery of buried treasure beneath the Chapel floor. It was here that a schoolboy discovered the fabulous hoard of Pictish silver while helping with excavations in 1958. The story of the treasure is just part of the history of St Ninian's Isle, but one that enthrals the visitor when told inside the Chapel against the backdrop of the silver sand tombolo with the sparkling blue ocean on either side. Despite their promise to return it to Shetland, the National Museums of Scotland keep the St Ninian's Isle treasure in Edinburgh, well away from the context of the find. There have been many attempts to have it returned to its rightful home for display in the Shetland Museum, only to be met by intransigence. When recounting this story to my guests I would often refer to the St Ninian's Isle treasure as being Shetland's Elgin Marbles. On one occasion I had to look away and contain myself when someone commented in agreement: "Aye, thae Elgin Marbles shuid gae back tae Elgin!"

Shaggy dog story

I wasn't the only guide at St Ninian's Isle. There was Sid. Sid was a dog that lived in the farmhouse at the top of the track leading down to the sand tombolo. He would accompany us all the way across, sometimes he would ask us to play fetch with him by bringing thick stalks of kelp to throw. Other times he would see us all the way over to the Isle and onto the path leading to the Chapel, then hurry back to the sand to assist someone else. Sometimes he'd be waiting on the sand to accompany us back. He soon got to know my minibus and if he wasn't at the sand when we arrived he would come loping down the field from the house to greet us. He was on the sand when I did my first official tour with two ladies from London and he was still on duty when I did my last tour before retiring. All my guests loved Sid. Many said they wished they could take him home with them. Sid is a true ambassador for Shetland.

Sid. Tour guide and ambassador for Shetland.

Stranger on the shore

Not all my visits to St Ninian's Isle were in blazing sunshine. Sometimes there'd be rain and strong winds, when a quick walk onto the sand tombolo would be sufficient for all but the hardiest. On one occasion thick banks of sea fog were rolling in across the island bringing visibility down to just a few tens of metres. I'd walked over to the Chapel with a small group and as we were walking back I was telling them about the unpopular 19th century laird, known as the "Wickid Laird", who owned the island and the crofting lands of Bigton and Ireland opposite. In those days crofting tenants were compelled to fish for the laird as part of their tenancy agreement. Because the laird provided the boats and lines, he also owned the fish that his tenants caught.

One winter, after a bad summer harvest, there was a shortage of flour causing near famine among his tenants. In desperation the tenants used the boats to surreptitiously catch fish to exchange for meal (flour) with merchants in Scalloway. When the laird found out he doubled their rents. One December day a year later, a boat with his tenants was fishing off the southwest corner of the Isle when their attention was drawn to the shore by a gunshot. They saw a well-dressed man scrambling over a point of rocks in the sea trying to retrieve a bird that he'd shot. A man dressed in the garb of a 19th-century gentleman on the Isle could only be the laird. As they watched a large wave broke and swept across the rocky point in a welter of foam. When the boiling surf cleared he'd vanished. No one in the boat was willing to risk going close to the rocks with a big swell running to search for the man, especially if the man was the Wickid Laird, so they carried on fishing. On their return the news of the laird's demise spread like wildfire across the crofting toonships; bottles were opened and Yule celebrations began early.

Alas, celebrations were premature. The laird appeared. The well-dressed gentleman they'd seen washed away wasn't the Wickid Laird, it was his children's private tutor who'd been out shooting birds. The laird was not amused. A legal enquiry was ordered and the fishermen were accused of failing to try to rescue the man despite the risk to them. Not only that, it was suggested the men may have killed and robbed the tutor. Sometime later the tutor's body washed ashore on a nearby island with all his gentleman's clothes and possessions intact. The fishermen were cleared of all responsibility and acquitted.

I'd just finished telling my guests this story as we stood in the swirling fog above the track leading up from the shore to the Chapel graveyard. By now the fog had got thicker and there was a distinct chill in the air. Suddenly a figure appeared out of the gloom and walked past us without word or acknowledgement, then disappeared again in the direction of the old graveyard. There was a moment's stunned silence, then my guests broke out in spontaneous applause and someone said, "Hey, that was well timed, who's your friend?"

The man that emerged from the fog sported a handlebar moustache, was dressed all over in a green tweed suit comprising a deerstalker hat, long double-breasted buttoned jacket, plus-fours, matching socks and leather brogues. Every inch the dress you'd expect of a 19th century gentleman. I had great difficulty trying to convince my companions that this was no set up, purely a coincidence. It was just a chance meeting with an eccentrically-dressed tourist I'd never seen before (or since).

Ley line seeker

Another foggy experience was with a German gentleman. He'd been visiting as many of Shetland's standing stones as he could by bicycle, but our wind and hilly topography were taking their toll on his legs. He booked me for a tour to West Mainland to see the alignment of the small standing stones heading for Culswick broch. He explained that his visit to Shetland was part of his investigation of ley lines across Europe. If I understood him correctly he believed that ley lines were pathways our prehistoric ancestors could use to guide them great distances across the landscape.

Following our visit to Culswick he expressed a wish to visit the Neolithic axe factory at the Beorgs of Uyea in Mainland's empty quarter to the north of Ronas Hill. The axe factory is actually an area of small quarry sites where our Neolithic ancestors worked narrow igneous dykes of blue-green felsite into polished tools some four thousand years ago. The site he wanted to visit is about five kilometres from the main road, mostly along a rough track followed by a traverse across a boulder-strewn hillside. I pointed this out to my guest, but as it was his last day in Shetland he was keen to visit the site. The day was wearing on and cloud was lowering onto the hills. Fortunately we were using my small four-by-four jeep so I could save time by driving along the rough track.

I had visited the axe factory probably about two or three times before in my life but hadn't been there for a few years. My normal route was to leave the rough track at a bend in the track above Mill Loch, then traverse almost two kilometres across the hillside to the ruins of a Bronze Age chambered cairn and onward to the axe factory. When we got to spot where I intended to leave the jeep we found the Beorgs completely shrouded in hill fog with visibility less than a couple of hundred metres. Not having a compass with me the sensible and safe thing to do was to abandon the exercise. However, as it was his only chance to visit the site my companion persuaded me to make an attempt at guiding him through the fog. I didn't think I could find the cairn or the axe factory, but I agreed to try on the proviso that if I missed it and we found ourselves on the track at the far side of the Beorgs we'd abandon our search and return along the track.

We set off and picked our way in eerie silence across the boulder-strewn hillside in a swirling grey circle of fog. I tried to walk as straight a line as possible by keeping the ground sloping away to my right, knowing by doing so that we wouldn't get lost. After what seemed an interminable time I suddenly saw a dark mass looming out of the fog right in front of me. It was the remains of the chambered cairn, we'd walked straight to it. From there we continued on in the same vein in what I hoped was the right direction. Just as I was beginning to think we'd missed it, we stumbled on the main working chamber of the axe factory. On arriving at our destination I expressed surprise in the fact we'd walked directly to the chambered cairn and found the axe factory. My German seeker of ley lines was not in the least bit surprised; by his reasoning we'd just been following a path determined by a ley line.

Neolithic "Axe Factory" at the Beorgs of Uyea, North Roe. The blue-green felsite rock was quarried, shaped and polished to make "knives" and axes.

Stanydale seer

Although not totally dismissive, I have a high degree of scepticism regarding paranormal events. My mother certainly believed in predictive dreams or second sight. I'm happy for people to believe anything they wish, provided they don't impose their beliefs on the freedoms of others. My scepticism was sorely tested on a day when I took a visitor to the so called "temple" at Stanydale in West Mainland. Situated about one kilometre from the road, and completely surrounded by moorland hills, Stanydale is a prehistoric site first occupied about four thousand years ago when, in addition to Neolithic dwelling houses, a larger building was constructed nearby. The houses and the larger building were excavated in 1949 by archaeologist C.S.T. Calder who interpreted the megalithic structure as a temple or meeting hall.

I first visited Stanydale when I was planning my tour itineraries. I knew it existed and that it was a prehistoric building but I'd never read up on it or researched it. One autumn evening I was driving past the area so I thought I'd walk up to the site to see if it was a possibility for inclusion in my tour itineraries. Walking towards the east facing Temple doorway there appears to be a processional route marked by standing stones that are aligned with the rising and setting sun at the equinox. Stanydale Temple is impressive, even allowing for post-excavation restorations. In the quiet evening light of my first visit it certainly had an atmosphere. It gave me a kind of *déjà vu* feeling that I'd been somewhere like this before. It put me in mind of the huge Neolithic temple of Xantia on the Maltese island of Gozo that Ann and I had visited earlier that year. What I didn't know at the time was that Calder had concluded: *"it is almost impossible not to assume that the Maltese temples are the prototypes from which Stanydale is derived and which solve the question of its purpose."* Coincidence? This conclusion by Calder is no longer considered valid by archaeologists.

One morning in late March in my second year of guiding, I got a call from a lady staying in self-catering accommodation in Lerwick. She booked me to take her husband out on a tour as her birthday treat for him. I duly collected him from Lerwick, and because he'd never been to West Mainland we did a tour to Waas and all points west. He was a pleasant, quiet-spoken chap in his thirties and reasonably chatty, but didn't say much about himself and his wife other that they were from the south of England. On our way back we were passing the sign for Stanydale Temple and I asked if he'd like a walk across the moor to the site. He readily agreed and we walked up towards the Temple. At that time there were no interpretation panels at the Neolithic house or the Temple other than the information on the gate. He seemed strangely quiet until we were about a hundred metres or so from the Temple when he stopped and asked if I minded if he told me something. Of course I said I didn't mind, what was it? To my utter surprise he told me that he was psychic, and the area we were in was having a big effect on him. Not only that, he went on to say that he was able to see people from the past walking about on the site.

I was stunned into silence not knowing what to say to this revelation. If I hadn't been in his company all day, along with the fact that he'd made this statement in a calm and serious manner, I'd probably have decried such notions and scanned the horizon for men in white coats. I guess he could see my shock and went on to say that he didn't want to worry me, but if I wished he would describe to me what he could see. Recovering my composure and now overcome by curiosity I said that I'd be happy for him to relate whatever visions he was having. What followed was probably one of the most remarkable half-hours or so of my tour-guiding experience. Before we entered the Temple he pointed to the hill behind and said he could see a large fire burning on top. He then described a line of people making their way from the Temple up the hill towards it. We entered the Temple and walked through to the inner chamber. He turned and looked back and described two men in cloaks carrying spears standing in the inner chamber by the entrance passageway. I don't think I was able to say much about the Temple to him other than relate its age and its excavation history which he didn't know.

When we left the Temple he pointed to more people, that only he could see, approaching us on a pathway from the direction of the standing stones. On the way back to the road we stopped at the site of the Neolithic house excavation. Here he said that he could see a girl with long dark hair just below the entrance to the house where she was taking a fish out of a fish pond. Even today I don't know what to make of this experience. He described these activities at Stanydale in quiet, matter-of-fact conversational tones, as if, as an observer, he didn't wish to disturb anyone. I'm sure that he believed he was seeing what he described and I don't think he was on a mission to convince me of his psychic powers. It was only much later when looking at my diary that I realised we'd been there on March 20th, the day of the vernal equinox.

Sun setting behind Stanydale Temple, West Mainland.
Photo © David Gifford Photography.

Fit the Eighth:
"As ithers see us"

"Lerwick is a dirty little town with very hospitable simple inhabitants. Main Street was designed by a man with a squint builded on the lines of a corkscrew."

This was how a visitor to Shetland described Lerwick in his diary. In a letter to his mother he tells of a fight between whalers in the town's Queen's Hotel then says: *"Lerwick is the town of crooked streets and ugly maidens and fish. A most dismal hole, with two hotels and one billiard table. Country round is barren and ugly. No trees in the island."*

Going ashore for bait for handline fishing in a voe north of Lerwick, he noted in his diary: *"Such dismal hovels, the esquimaux have better houses. Each has a little square hole in the ceiling to let out the smoke of a large peat fire in the middle of the room. They were all civil enough. Met one pretty but shy girl even in this barbarous spot."*

These quotes from Arthur Conan Doyle tell us how he saw Shetland on his first visit to the islands. In the spring of 1880 he'd taken time off from his medical studies in Edinburgh to ship out as a surgeon on the sealer/whaler *Hope* of Peterhead bound for the Arctic. He spent ten days in Lerwick while the ship signed on about fifty Shetlanders for the voyage.

I've had as my guests people from every continent and from most European countries. Outside Europe, most came from Australia, New Zealand, USA and Canada with a few from India. Students came mainly from Europe, China and Japan. I also had the pleasure of meeting one student from Argentina and another from Brazil.

My best reward from tour guiding was meeting people from different cultures and spending enough time in their company to see Shetland and our culture through their eyes. Sometimes with amusing consequences. One question often asked was "Why do you have graves by the roadsides?" Not such a daft question

Lerwick Main Street in 1880; "builded on the lines of a corkscrew". Photo © Shetland Museum.

perhaps, as in some countries there are shrines set up along roads in memory of tragic deaths of workers constructing highways. What my guests were seeing was actually tombstone-shaped markers for water mains and telephone cables.

Often mistaken for headstones.

A town called toilets

I've never been to Japan, but like most people I had heard of their emphasis on politeness and rules of etiquette. I'd met Japanese people socially and through work before, but spending a whole day guiding Japanese tourists was a different and rewarding experience. Most of my Japanese guests were usually postgraduate students attending British universities so their spoken English was very good indeed.

On one occasion I took a group of four student girls on a tour of North Mainland. This tour took us on side-roads leading northeast to Ollaberry, then to Collafirth and back along the coast of Ronas Voe to Urafirth and on to Hillswick. It was pretty much a standard tour with photo stops, explanations and my answers to their questions. They were a happy group of friends that chatted away amongst themselves in their own language most of the time. I noticed after a while that each time we stopped at road junctions they would comment to each other then giggle. After this happened a few times I just had to find out to what the joke was they were sharing.

The next time it happened I remarked to the lead girl that I was happy that they were enjoying the tour, but I was puzzled at what was amusing them at the road junctions.

They all became a little embarrassed at this, then eventually one said, "It is the name of your town we find amusing, it is on all the road signs. That is the town you are taking us to, ne?"

I still hadn't twigged, thinking perhaps that Ollaberry was something rude in Japanese, so I asked her what was the name of the town they found so strange.

"Toilets," was her blushing reply.

I had to explain as best I could that our local government attached the same style of sign indicating the location of public toilets on signposts as those pointing to the villages in the area.

Pointing the way to a town called Toilets?

What's in a name?

Set in the scenic landscape of Esha Ness against the spectacular backdrop of St Magnus Bay, Tangwick Haa Museum was a favourite stop for my guests, and for me. Often I would let my guests wander to enjoy the exhibits while I chatted to whichever of the duty curators was at the reception desk. During tours I would talk to my guests in my best English or toned down dialect, but when chatting directly with the curator we'd both lapse into full-on dialect.

On one occasion I noticed that our conversation had captured the attention of an American lady. "Aw surre don't know whawt y'awll arre sayin, but Aw surre do like thaw way you is sayin it," she observed in her broad Southern drawl.

Tangwick Haa Museum. Always a "pot of gold" experience here for visitors. Photo (c) Eileen Mullay.

Having no foreign language skills, and being the product of an education that taught none, I was indeed fortunate that almost all my guests spoke fluent or near fluent English. However the English language does sometimes throw up some ridiculous contradictions to catch out the foreign visitor. Driving into Lerwick a Swiss student asked me if how far was it to the railway station. I explained that we had no trains or railway transport in Shetland.

"Oh, but I saw as sign for it back there?" she said.

Puzzled, I asked what exactly did the sign say.

"Train Shetland."

Train Shetland is the Vocational Training Centre at Shetland College.

Many tours were booked through direct contact with me by email. In most cases I didn't need the guest's home address, just their arrival date in Shetland and the accommodation address of their stay. From the guest's name and

That way to the trains?

email address it was sometimes too easy to make a wrong assumption about the person. One girl made bookings for tours with me during a Shetland Folk Festival weekend. Her email domain was *.il* and she had an Irish sounding of name Karen More so I assumed *.il* was for Ireland. Wrong, *.il* is the domain for Israel. This girl was a folk music fan from Tel Aviv. The few days she came on tours and guided walks with me were very sunny and windy, as is often the case in early May. She was very pale skinned and her face was showing the reddening effects. I commented that her family would be surprised when she returned to Tel Aviv with a tan. She explained that she didn't go out in the sun in Tel Aviv much because the sun was so harsh and hot, but she liked the Shetland sun because, in comparison, it was "just so soft!"

Someone with an American Online (*.aol*) email address can be from any country. When I took an *.aol* email booking from a geology student with the name Tracy Martin I assumed it was from an American girl. I'd arranged to collect this guest from Islesburgh Youth Hostel and went there at the agreed time. About five minutes or so after the appointed time there was no sign of anyone other than an Indian lad sitting on a bench outside the hostel. I asked him if he was staying there and if he had seen an American girl called Tracy.

"I'm Tracy Martin."

It turned out that he came from Goa, so had a Portuguese surname. His parents had chosen to give him the uncommon boy's name of Tracy.

In Shetland's recent past it was not uncommon to find Christian names for males and females to be borrowed from the Bible; Hercules and Tamar (pronounced Ta-mir) being common at one time. So when I received an email from a lady called Tamar in Chicago I wondered briefly if there was a Shetland connection. I soon realised there wasn't after she introduced herself as "Tay-mar", with a very Jewish surname. She was a very nice lady and wife of an internationally renowned surgeon who had private practices in Chicago and London. She'd come to Shetland for a few days while her husband was working in London. Her visit to Shetland was at the time that a Barack Obama from Chicago was running for President for the first time. She and another guest were chatting about American politics and, knowing she was from Chicago, I made a remark in jest to lighten the conversation: "I guess you'll know the Obamas then?"

"Yes, actually I do."

It turned out that Barack and Michelle Obama lived next door but one to her.

Dangerous liaisons

I made myself a rule that as far as possible as a tour guide I would not get involved in conversations or express opinions about politics, religion or race, especially those of guests. Only rarely did I have guests that expressed strong opinions on those subjects, and although not always agreeing, I always kept my own counsel. Sometimes an innocent remark can spark a strong reaction. Two very nice ladies from California had been on a few outings with me and we'd stopped for lunch at a cafe. Someone had discarded a newspaper on a chair by our table. The front page had pictures side by side of Prime Minister Tony Blair and President George W. Bush. One lady picked up the paper and without thinking I casually remarked that her President had made the front page. Her reply came with some venom.

"Bush is not _my_ President, if he was here and I had a gun I'd shoot him dead!"

She was serious, and she worked in a District Attorney's office.

I'd often be asked if we have dangerous creatures in Shetland such as snakes and venomous spiders, which we don't. However most folk don't ask, and many assume that we do. I was driving a group that included an Australian couple on a tour of North Mainland and we'd stopped for lunch at Braewick Cafe. I'd left the minibus window a little open and when we returned a large crane-fly, known as locally as Daddy-long-legs, had found its way in and was on the windscreen. I just casually mentioned that we'd got a Daddy-long-legs as an extra passenger. This remark brought screams of "Get it out!" from the Australian lady. Daddy-long-legs is apparently a species of large spider in Australia.

Another group I had on tour included a lady from Florida who gave herself quite a scare. We'd stopped by a sand spit called The Blade, by the shore of Ronas Voe, for everyone to stretch their legs and take photos of the red granite cliffs of the fjord. Suddenly there was a shout of "Snake, snake!" from this lady who was walking backwards pointing to a patch of long grass. I walked over and casually picked up a black, wizened up, stalk of kelp and presented her with her snake.

Snake in the grass?

Students

Over the years I had several small groups of students, usually from mainland China, booking tours with me. Most had been through our university system and were now postgraduate students working for Masters Degrees. Generally, they seemed to have no desire to go home during university holidays but join together as a group to travel to various parts of the British Isles. I got the impression they had rich parents funding their studies; most seemed to carry top of the range photographic equipment which would bear this theory out. Like the Japanese they made happy and entertaining groups.

A girl from mainland China and her boyfriend booked me for a few tours during their stay. I would pick them up each morning from the Lerwick Hotel and take them on a tour. She was a sociology student and asked a lot of questions about life in Shetland and how our local services were run and how things had changed over the years. Just in conversation she asked if I had any siblings. I said that I didn't, then without thinking asked if she had any brothers and sisters. "No," she said, "it was not allowed."

A Japanese student and her mother came on a tour of North Mainland. The student had to translate between me and the mother; this arrangement worked out fine and they seemed to enjoy the tour. The girl was particularly interested in Shetland history and what we did in winter. I explained that unlike summer, in mid-winter our daylight hours were few and it was dark between mid-afternoon and mid-morning. In the late afternoon we were driving back through the long stretch of moorland between Voe and Lerwick known as the Lang Kames. The girl said something to her mother then said to me that she was glad to be here in the summer as we wouldn't be able to drive along this road in the winter. I replied that winter wasn't a problem as we didn't get much snow to stop us driving. She said that she meant that it would be too dark to drive on this road since there were no street lights. This stumped me for a bit, and I asked if they didn't drive in the dark in Japan. She said that it is never dark in Japan because all the roads have street lights and there is neon advertising and lights everywhere. I showed her the headlights on the minibus and explained that we used them for driving in the dark. She was genuinely astonished; she had no idea that car headlights could be used in this way and just assumed that they were there just so you could see another car approaching.

In contrast, I have had students from Russia as my guests on only two occasions. One was a girl doing her second degree at Cambridge. Not only did she speak English fluently but four other European languages as well. She'd brought her parents over from Moscow. As they were touring the whole of Scotland in just one week, they wished to see as much of Shetland as possible in one day. I collected them at 8am when they disembarked from the Aberdeen ferry and delivered them to Sumburgh airport at 7pm. In that time we toured the whole of Northmaven and Esha Ness then Scalloway and the South Mainland, including Sumburgh Head, clad with puffins, just before they departed. All day Shetland had been at its sunny, summer best with hardly any wind. Near the end of the tour the father had a bit of a conversation his daughter who had been interpreting for her parents. I asked if anything was the matter. "No," she said. "He thinks your island is just so great, he doesn't want to leave."

Cruise ships

When I began tour guiding the port of Lerwick hosted between 40-50 cruise ships of all sizes each year. In 2018 the port will host over 90 ships carrying 92,000 passengers. During my time as tour operator I would take email bookings from independent travellers planning their visit from these ships. Generally these were small groups of six to eight who wanted a more individual and different experience from that offered by large coach tours. The majority of those booking in this way were American and Canadian, although I did have a family of seven from Mexico City as my guests on one tour of South Mainland. The teenage children in this family in particular had done a fair bit of research and asked a lot of intelligent questions about all aspects of Shetland. This was very much an enjoyable educational tour for them but they did find the mild Shetland summer day a bit chilly.

Usually just eight hours in port, cruise ships run on a tight schedule of arrival and departure times so I had to be mindful of the fact that a late return would result in my guests missing the ship. With this in mind I always factored in a return time that would allow for any unexpected holdups on the tour. Fortunately this never happened. I had a booking from a group of Canadians who requested a short tour of the South Mainland followed by a walk across the St Ninian's Isle tombolo then around the coast to the other side of the Isle and back again. It was a nice sunny day and we completed the walk around the Isle; unfortunately I hadn't factored in the unusually high spring tide. When we got back to the tombolo the Atlantic had decided to cross it in a couple of places, a quite unusual event in summer on a day with little wind or swell. Of course it wasn't possible to wait for the tide to turn so it was shoes and socks off for everybody and wade. Fortunately the water was no more than ankle deep and my guests viewed being potentially marooned as a bit of an adventure.

Most visitors who book independently do a lot of research on the places they'd like to visit when in Shetland, but some don't and just follow the standard Shetland guff churned out by the cruise companies. From those unaware of the scale our islands I would sometimes get requests to visit all these, in just a few hours: Muckle Flugga, Mousa, Scalloway Castle, St Ninian's Isle, Clickimin and Jarlshof, also I must include Shetland ponies and "Someburg puffins". In reply I would always offer my guests a choice of either a North Mainland itinerary or a South Mainland itinerary. The north tour would take in Tingwall, Pettadale, Voe, Mavis Grind, Ronas Voe, Braewick Cafe, Esha Ness cliffs and Tangwick Haa Museum. South would include Clickimin, Scalloway, St Ninian's Isle, Jarlshof and Sumburgh Head. Photo stops were included for flora and fauna as and whenever we encountered it.

The maximum number I could take in my minibus was eight passengers. Sometimes a group of four travelling together on a cruise would book a tour then recruit another four from the ship to share the cost. One group had recruited a lady who, although well meaning, was starting to annoy most of the others on the tour. Every time someone asked me a question she would chip in with an answer before I could speak. This was okay up to a point, but more often than not what she was saying was misleading or wrong, then I would have to reply in such a way as not to make her appear a complete idiot. I could sense that the others in the group were getting a bit fed up with her interjections so I had to think of a diplomatic way to ease the growing tension in the group.

My opportunity came when we were passing a field that was snow-white with thousands of plants gently waving in the breeze. Someone asked what the plant was and for once the lady didn't have an answer. I explained that this plant was called "Lukki's oo" in Shetland and the English name was bog cotton.

"Not possible," she interjected loudly. "You can't have cotton here, it's far too cold, that ain't cotton, this ain't Alabama!"

I saw my chance and countered by asking her if she had heard of the pharmaceutical company called Johnson and Johnson.

"Yes," she said, "a good ol' American company."

Then I asked if she'd ever used their packets of cotton buds.

"Oh yes, all the time."

"Well," I said, pointing to the acre or so of white blobs on stalks waving in the breeze, "this is where they grow them."

There was complete silence for a few seconds. I thought perhaps I'd gone too far, and then the whole group exploded into laughter. Thankfully the lady joined in. She still asked me questions and chatted during the rest of the tour but thankfully she had got the message and didn't interject by answering the questions of others.

Growing cotton buds?

I had an email request from a young American lady for a private tour for just her and her mother when their ship docked in Lerwick. Most folk from cruise ships are happy to share the tour and costs with others so this was an unusual request. I met them from the ship and we had a relaxed tour on one of the best summer days of the year. They seemed a perfectly usual mother and daughter having quality time together, no fancy clothes, makeup or cameras, but I wondered why they'd requested a private tour. The daughter was very excited about the tour, especially about Shetland ponies so I had to stop at each group of ponies we saw. Her mother explained that when the daughter was small she'd learned to ride on a Shetland pony they'd had on their ranch.

On the road out to Sumburgh Lighthouse a boulder that looks like a skull has been balanced on a rock near the road. On an earlier tour someone had remarked to me that the skull looked like Darth Vader from the *Star Wars* films. I stopped the minibus and jokingly pointed this out to the daughter.

She jumped out saying, "My hero, I must take his picture!"

While she was doing this her mother was laughing at her antics of trying to take a selfie photo with this boulder and remarked how relaxed and happy her daughter was on this tour and how much she was enjoying Shetland. Her mother was obviously very proud of her, so I asked what job her daughter had. She was a bit non-committal saying her daughter worked in the clothing industry. A few months later I was in a dentist's waiting room and a magazine was open where someone had left it on a chair. The same girl from the tour was looking up at me from the page. She is a top model with the women's international fashion house Victoria's Secret.

Darth Vader's skull?

Over the years folks who came on tours with me from off cruise ships came back to Shetland for longer stays having enjoyed their tour as sample of what Shetland had to offer. One larger group that I shared with James Tait of *Island Trails* liked us so much that they came back on another cruise the following year bearing us gifts from Texas. Such a positive feedback from guests is praise indeed.

Humours of Jarlshof

Although it represents four thousand years of human settlement the Jarlshof archaeological site covers a surprisingly small area. This is because each layer of building and settlement is superimposed one atop another. At Jarlshof I would guide my guests through the site's unique excavated timeline that has revealed each layer of settlement preserved beneath the shifting sands of the area. I would start at 2700 years BC in Neolithic Shetland then on through the Bronze and Iron Age houses and broch to the Viking and Norse settlements, ending at the 17th century laird's house. On cruise ship days the Jarlshof site is on the itinerary of the large coaches, so it wasn't uncommon to encounter three sixty-seat coaches there at the one time; bedlam on wheels. I'd built flexibility into my tour itinerary so that I could avoid Jarlshof until the coaches had departed, then take my guests around. Sometimes I'd endeavour to get there before coaches arrived.

Rather than just stand and lecture my groups I always tried to let them interact with the site. This I did by drawing parallels with the present, or by pointing to something and asking for their opinion. For example, most of the prehistoric houses on the site have the appearance of being dug well into the ground and I would ask why this should be. I would then explain that these houses were in fact built on the prehistoric ground surface and that it was centuries of periodic sand blow that had buried each layer of settlement. It was thanks to the drifting sand that Jarlshof is so well preserved. This method worked well and I always got a positive reaction from my guests, sometimes their responses could be amusing.

The division of the interior of Bronze and Iron Age roundhouses and wheelhouses into alcoves spark questions from visitors, questions that are often qualified by their 21st century lifestyles: "What were they for? Are these bedrooms?" In one wheelhouse alcove there is a large, upright, flat sandstone slab that one lady was convinced was a headboard from a bed.

There are quite a number of trough querns to be seen at various points associated with the Bronze and Iron Age roundhouses. These are large boulders hollowed out to resemble a deep trough, open at one end. Grain was put into the trough and ground into flour using a smaller stone. The number of querns found on the site demonstrates the reliance of all these past communities on grain production for the major component of their diet. Querns were used each day by those prehistoric people to grind flour to feed their families; the "daily grind" goes back a long way into prehistory. The first quern is found in a Bronze Age house. Here I would always start by asking my groups what they thought it was for. Most folk could work it out with a bit of encouragement, but there was one lady whose answer, I suspect, reflected a Hotel California lifestyle: "I know what that is," she said, "it's a foot spa."

Historic Environment Scotland, who own the Jarlshof site, have placed informative panels at various points along the timeline and these were useful stopping points for me in guiding my guests around. I did find it necessary on occasion to point out that illustrations on the panels take an idyllic view of life in our prehistory by planting a nuclear family of grandparents, parents and two-point-four children back in time. The rather strange panel illustration of the Iron Age broch showing a high-rise, multi-storey timber house inside a massive stone tower was often a talking point. Archaeologists reckon brochs were first built in Shetland and the design was copied in Orkney and in the north and west of

Iron Age bedroom?

Bronze Age foot spa.

Scotland. Often this would raise a laugh when it was pointed out that Shetland had lost its trees some two thousand years before brochs were built, so to design a building requiring massive timbers on a treeless island was a remarkable achievement. Even more remarkable would be finding the timber for over a hundred brochs that were built in Shetland.

Brochs are an archaeological enigma; no-one really knows their true purpose. There are many broch theories such as defensive food stores or watch towers. Favoured by some is the theory that a broch is a high status Iron Age chief's "castle" from which he would oversee and control the tribe. Answering visitors' questions is of course part of a tour guide's job and you soon learn to expect the unexpected. The open air sites of Jarlshof and Old Scatness could often get a bit noisy with planes and helicopters taking off, sometimes prompting the question, "Why did they build the brochs so near to the airport?"

The answer is, of course, "They were Iron Age control towers."

Further along the timeline, just by the steps to the Viking longhouses, is a near spherical boulder of gabbro almost the size of a football. It would have originated as a slab of rock torn from a mountain by a glacier and rounded by glacial transport and sediment-laden meltwater. This boulder is interesting due to the fact that it has been more heavily smoothed on one half of the sphere than on the other. Not only that, but gabbro is not found in the bedrock or glacial erratics of southern Shetland, the nearest gabbro is in the north part of Mainland. This boulder had to be brought to Jarlshof for use as a tool, perhaps brought by Vikings for working leather on, thus rubbing one half smooth. I was in the habit of pointing to this boulder and asking for opinions before giving my thoughts on its origin. One chap suggested jokingly that perhaps Vikings were into ten-pin bowling. A lady in the group took him literally and tried to turn it over in search of the finger holes.

Boulder of gabbro at Jarlshof. Possibly brought by Norse settlers.

Fit the Ninth: Memorable Folk and Faux Pas

There are no strangers here; only friends you haven't yet met.
(William Butler Yeats.)

If I had to have a maxim for being a Shetland tour guide I would borrow that quote from William Butler Yeats. The best part of tour guiding was the privilege of meeting such a wide range of people and some fascinating characters. Touring put me in the company of my guests for at least a full day, sometimes for three or four days, so we'd often have time to relax and chat about their backgrounds and what brought them to Shetland. Of course, chatting in this way could have its pitfalls. American radio talk show host Dennis Prager once said, *"Every person who speaks or writes for the public will make an occasional faux pas, and sooner or later will write or say something inappropriate."* And this I did on a few occasions when my mouth got out of sync with my brain.

Life's rich tapestry

My years of meeting people as a tour guide gave me an insight to the work of a whole range of different professions. Spending all day in the company of my guests gave me time to chat and discover a little about the jobs they did. A mother and daughter duo from London were spending just one day in Shetland and had booked a South Mainland tour. I had worked out that they worked together, so by way of conversation over lunch I asked what their occupation was. To my astonishment they ran a private detective agency. They explained that this occupation isn't as glamorous as depicted on TV; most of their work was civil cases involving legal aid. They did tell me that their most memorable case was finding and arranging the safe return of Arthur, from the cat food advertisement. Arthur was the star of the TV ad for Spillers Kattomeat, famous for eating the food straight out of the tin with his paw. He'd been kidnapped and held to ransom in 1974 but was reunited with his owners by their efforts and lived to the ripe old age of 16.

One day I got a call to pick up an American gentleman staying at the Queens Hotel in Lerwick who'd booked a North Mainland tour. It turned out he was the Deputy Sheriff of Dallas County (retired). A nice chap, with a deep Texas drawl, talked in short sentences. He had been retired for some time and carried a lot of excess weight, thus took up a goodly proportion of the double front seat in the minibus. In his prime he wouldn't have been a person to argue with in his professional capacity.

His first words to me were a bit worrying. "Hello son," he said. "If ya see me poppin pills don't worry, just gotta bit of a health problem."

I said that I was sorry to hear that, but I had to ask what the problem was just in case something happened on the tour.

"Too many forty-eight hour shifts livin' on coffee and cigarettes; my heart's done for."

We had a good tour and he liked what he saw but he was a bit short on conversation. On our way back, driving on the long, straight road through the Lang Kames, a couple of motorbikes screamed past us at about double our speed of 60mph. I passed a comment to the sheriff to the effect that those lads were in a bit of a hurry.

He looked ahead at the rapidly vanishing bikers. "Hell son," he drawled, "this island ain't big enough to be in that much of a hurry."

A lone traveller was a school teacher from Boston who had been to Shetland once before as a cruise ship passenger. This time she'd come for a week just to photograph croft houses, not modern ones, only abandoned and ruined ones. I never quite understood why she had this fascination with these buildings as she had no historical connection with Shetland. Her camera was film, not digital. She told me that she had her photos blown up to poster size to pin up on the walls of her apartment. For her to get photos of crofting townships I took her off the beaten track to some that had been empty and roofless since being cleared by the lairds in the 19th century.

One visit was to the deserted crofts of Grimsetter on the island of Bressay. Rather than risk my minibus on the kilometre of rough track that passed near the crofts, I suggested we walk across the hillside from the main road. I hadn't reckoned on the hillside being "bonxie city" in the nesting season. Unlike some other parts of Shetland, the birds on this hillside probably didn't see humans from one year to the next, and boy, did they let us know. One after the other they were queuing up to swoop, full speed, straight at us, head height. The attack from the bonxie squadron didn't bother me over much as I had a stick to hold aloft to divert their aim. Unfortunately my photographer guest freaked out and screamed. If someone had been filming us the result would have passed muster as a scene from Hitchcock's *The Birds*. The poor lass was terrified almost beyond reason. The only way I could get her to retrace our steps was to hold my jacket over her head. This way she could only see her feet then I could guide her back to the road. Safely in the minibus I apologised for taking her into the realm of the bonxie, but she was fine about it, it was just the unexpected viciousness of the attack that shocked her. In the end I did take the minibus along the track to Grimsetter and she got her photos.

The next day with the same photographer lady we'd returned to Lerwick as floats were queuing up for the mid-summer carnival. One float was bedecked with the Confederate flags of the one-time southern states of America. She was genuinely angered by this, asking if those people on the float really understood what that flag represented. To her it was comparable to displaying the Nazi flag in Britain. She explained that the Confederate flag had been used as a symbol of opposition to the Civil Rights movement and is now often used as a rallying symbol for white supremacist groups.

Shetland's tourist season is May to October so it was unusual to have any tour bookings during the winter months. It was in late January that I got a call from Busta Hotel near Brae, asking if I would be willing to take an Italian gentleman on a tour to some of the West and South Mainland and what would the price be. At that time diesel was nearly £1.50 per litre and I lived thirty-five miles from Brae, so round trips of picking him up and returning him to the hotel would add one hundred and forty miles onto the tour mileage. I worked out a price for the tour with this extra mileage in mind and let the hotel know. It came to be a substantial sum so I felt a little guilty about quoting a fairly large amount for just one person to pay. All was agreed and I drove to the hotel to pick him up. After introductions we chatted about his background. He told me that he originally came from a small village in northern Italy but now lived just outside Monaco where he kept his twenty-metre yacht. Any sense of guilt I had about the cost of the tour quickly vanished.

It turned out that he'd been a marine engineer and with his sons had set up the Marine Park in Malta, now one of its top tourist attractions. Recently they'd sold the business and he was now semi-retired. He'd just popped up to Shetland from London while his wife was doing a bit of shopping, just to see what it was like and perhaps buy some Fair Isle knitwear for her birthday. About lunchtime we were in Scalloway and he suggested we have a bar lunch in the hotel there. This was okay by me. In the bar we were browsing the menu, him with a large malt whisky, me with a ginger beer, when he noticed lobster on the specials board. He asked me if I'd like to share a lobster with him, quickly adding that he'd pay. Knowing it would be rude to refuse, I agreed. Two large whiskies (him) and a ginger beer (me) later, the lobster arrived. Meanwhile he'd told me a bit more about himself.

As well as their home in Monaco, he explained how they'd bought a penthouse in Paris with a view of the Eiffel Tower. They had it refurbished and redesigned by a top architect in a modern minimalist style. Apparently they had a bit of difficulty getting the three-metre long bronze table up to the top of the building! He went on to tell me that the gable of their new penthouse overlooked the River Seine, but, much to his wife's disappointment, there was no window for this view. He'd asked the architect to install a gable window, but was told that this was impossible due to strict planning laws in such a major conservation area. However, the architect had suggested a cunning plan. If they applied for permission to put a window in the gable they would be refused immediately. On the other hand, if they said nothing but went ahead and put a window in, and made it look very old, they could apply to have it removed and bricked up. This would be immediately refused and they would have their window. His wife got her view over the Seine.

One year in early May when I was getting ready for a busy season I had a phone call from South Queensland, Australia. The call was from an elderly sheep farmer who was hoping to visit Shetland with his wife in June and would like some tour details. I said that my tour calendar for June was quite busy but if he gave me some dates I'd give him some details and availability days.

"Not this year mate, next year," was the reply.

He was certainly planning ahead. I offered to email my tour descriptions.

"Email! No mate, we're lucky to have a phone out here."

We corresponded by post and phone, then in June the following year they came to Shetland. I'd arranged to collect them from Islesburgh Hostel in Lerwick. On the day I recognised them instantly. They were waiting for me outside the entrance; an elderly couple both dressed in their Sunday best, apart from the one thing nobody but an Australian sheep farmer would wear - his hat. She'd obviously kitted him out for their UK holiday; everything he was wearing was brand new, and not the everyday dress of a South Queensland sheep farmer, apart from that hat. It was a wide-brimmed leather hat, dark and mottled with countless years of sweat and wool lanolin, possibly nearly as old as him. I surmised that not even a holiday on the other side of the world can part an Australian sheep farmer and his hat.

The tour was through North Mainland. She was delighted in the scenery so different from South Queensland, and he in the multicoloured Shetland sheep. We'd had lunch in the Braewick Cafe and were on the road towards Esha Ness lighthouse and cliffs when we saw a marquee in a field. Cars were parked all along the road, men and dogs were in the field; this was the day of the Northmavine sheepdog trials. It was obvious to my guests what was going on.

"We gotta come back this way mate?" he asked.

She was glaring daggers at him, obviously having read his mind. I told him we'd be coming back along this road in a couple of hours.

"Mind if I hop out mate, and you pick me up on the way back?" said the only South Queensland sheep farmer ever to attend the Northmavine sheepdog trials. We picked him up on the way back; he'd had a good day.

Sometimes I was asked what religions are followed in Shetland and I would list many of the various denominations we have. I would often point out interesting church buildings and occasionally I'd be asked to give guests directions to a church of whichever denomination they followed. Not being absolutely accurate in this regard led to one of my most embarrassing moments as a tour guide. I'd taken a nice elderly couple on a tour of North Mainland. During the tour they'd told me they were of the Mormon faith and had recently returned from spreading the word in China.

Near the end of the day they asked if I knew of a Mormon church in Lerwick. I had it in my mind that I'd seen in the local press a story about a Mormon church opening in Shetland. I'd also noticed in passing that a new church had been built near the main road through Tingwall, not far from Lerwick. I put two and two together and said that I would show them where it was on our way back to Lerwick. At Tingwall I pulled into the car park in front of the church, just below a legend written in large letters on the wall. It didn't read as I expected (Church of Jesus Christ of Latter-day Saints), instead it read Kingdom Hall of Jehovah's Witnesses. My putting two and two together had just combined two of the world's religions. Thankfully they saw the funny side of the whole episode.

One middle-aged couple I had the pleasure of guiding for three days came from the north of England. Shetland was their last stop on a tour of Scotland and Orkney. From their conversations I realised that early on in the holiday the husband had left something important behind at one of their stops. Every time we moved on from a photo stop or cafe she would remind him of this, as I suspect she'd being doing for most of the previous week. At the end of their last day I dropped them and their luggage off at the Aberdeen-bound ferry, said my goodbyes and drove off. Just as I was about to leave the ferry terminal onto the main road I noticed something sticking out beneath the front passenger seat. It was the handle of her handbag she'd left under the seat. It contained all their money and their tickets for the ferry. I did a quick u-turn and caught up with them at the ticket desk and held up the handbag. The look of pure joy on his face and the total embarrassment on hers was a picture to behold.

It's a small world

Thanks to the BBC TV series *Shetland*, featuring the Fair Isle-born detective with the highly improbable name of Jimmy Perez, recognisable locations around Shetland have become photo stops for visiting fans. One of these is at Craigie's Stane by the Lodberrie on Lerwick's waterfront; Perez's fictional house. At this locality I often tell my guests that a creator of a much more interesting fictional detective visited Lerwick in 1880. This was of course Arthur Conan Doyle, when he arrived on the whaler *Hope*. I read out Doyle's quotes about Lerwick and ask my guests to guess the author. One guest immediately worked out who I was quoting and said her great-grandfather from Fraserburgh had been on the *Hope* with Doyle.

On my guided walks I carried on my belt a useful multi-pocket pouch made from Cordura by the travel products company Lifeventure. One day I was guiding a mixed group on a walk along the Esha Ness cliffs when a lady asked if I found the pouch useful. I replied that I found it extremely versatile and hard wearing; I could carry a small camera, mobile phone, keys and such like in it.

"Good," she said, "glad you like it, I designed it."

At the end of the trip I was collecting payment for the tour and giving change when my old wallet, of many years service, fell apart. As a joke I said to the lady that perhaps she could design and make a wallet from the same material as the pouch.

"Yes, I will," she said, and wrote down details of size and features I'd like in a wallet.

I thought no more of it until a couple of months later a wallet arrived in the post.

Lifeventure had added a new product to their line.

One morning I collected a girl from her hotel and another from the Tourist Centre. They'd never met before but when they got to chatting they discovered that each lived in London. Even more surprising was that both worked for the same company, had the same boss and the offices they worked in were on opposite sides of the same street. By pure chance they'd both taken the same week off, travelled to Shetland and booked on the same tour with me on the same day.

On another occasion two couples were on a tour. They'd never met before but the lady from one couple and the husband of the other both worked in different branches of the same well-known Scottish bank. They knew people in common and were exchanging stories about the ongoing banking crisis at the time and about the infamous CEO of this bank. Apparently the CEO was in the habit of dropping in, unannounced, on bank branches anywhere in the country to inspect them. A week or so before a visit he would send his PA undercover to the area to find out in which shops the bank staff bought lunchtime sandwiches, just to check if they stocked his favourite fillings. On one occasion the shop used by the branch staff sussed out what the undercover PA was up to and let a girl on the bank staff know. Thus the branch was alerted that a visit from their CEO was imminent and was ready for him. When the CEO found out how they'd been alerted he sacked the girl on the branch staff who had told her colleagues. I was glad to read just recently that the CEO had been stripped of his knighthood.

I don't have a great memory for names but I always seem to remember a face. A lady from Manchester and her family booked a tour with me and after a while I was sure that I'd met her somewhere before. It turned out she was called Rosemary and was originally from Lerwick; we'd both worked at the fish factory away back in 1969.

Another time when I was guiding a group from England on a geology field week I thought a lady in the group looked vaguely familiar. On the ferry back from Unst onto Yell she asked if I knew of a place on Yell called Heath Cottage as she'd stayed there as a fourteen-year-old on a family holiday. I said I did, and if she sat in the front seat I would point it out as we passed. Once we'd driven past and she'd recognised it, I asked if she remembered a small boy who used to bring eggs and milk from the croft down the road. She said she did. I replied that she was now sitting next to him.

I was asked by a family in Lerwick to take an Australian on a tour of the North Mainland. This chap had the broadest Aussie accent you can imagine so I felt obliged to speak in my tour-guide English. After about an hour we'd stopped at one of my viewpoints by the shore on Olna Firth where he asked a few questions about a laird that had owned the land in the area. Then he looked up at Clubb of Mulla behind us and said that he could remember being on that hilltop as a child at the Coronation Day bonfire. He'd been born not far from there and had emigrated to Australia as a young man. After that I just spoke to him in my normal dialect. As the tour went on his native tongue gradually returned, and by the end of the day, although he probably didn't notice, he sounded as if he'd never been away.

The uninhabited island of Hildasay, just west of Scalloway, had a quarry that was operational during the 19th century. Blocks of granite were transported from the quarry by bogies running on a railway track to a natural deep-water quay for shipment. The granite (actually granodiorite) was used for decorative building stone in Shetland and Scotland. Clipper ships bound for Australia for cargoes of wool topped off their ballast with blocks of Hildasay granite which could be sold on arrival there. Legend has it that the lintels of Melbourne Town Hall are fashioned from Hildasay granite. I would sometimes remark on this to my Australian guests, suggesting that the next time they were in that building they could chip off a bit from a lintel and post it to me for verification. None ever did. However, one Australian lady said that when they built their first house they salvaged granite blocks from an old wool packing station to make steps. These blocks were supposed to have come from a Scottish island. I took her to see some Hildasay granite on the Scalloway waterfront; although not definitive, she said it did look similar in colour to their steps.

The most remarkable person I ever had the privilege of guiding had himself been a tour guide, but, as I was to find out, at a quantum level higher than anything ever I'd done. A Lerwick guest house had called me on his behalf one evening to book a tour and I went to collect him the next morning. A white-haired, white-bearded man of medium build waited for me on the pavement. He was dressed in a dark brown cord jacket, best described as well travelled, with jumper and dark fawn trousers of similar vintage; shoes, no socks. His weather-beaten face had a rugged character suggestive of a life outdoors.

He opened the passenger door and introduced himself. "My name," he said, "is Pierre de Saint Julian Macbeth, but I'm Scotty to my friends."

I resisted the temptation to ask him to beam himself aboard the minibus.

That morning as we drove north through the Lang Kames to Voe I learned a bit about Scotty Macbeth. He told me that he was seventy-nine years old and from Carmel, California. He'd qualified as a field geologist and had his own business. He was also a bit of adventurer; he'd been one of the crew of a yacht that had won a Sydney to Hobart yacht race. He was most interested in the landscape we were driving through, especially when I told him Shetland's hills were the roots of an ancient mountain chain, once as high as the Himalaya. In 1962 he'd sold his business in California and joined the first American expedition to climb Mount Everest in 1963. I asked him if he'd got to the top; he said that he hadn't as he'd just been one of the support team. He told me that after the 1963 expedition, "My buddies and I liked it so much there that we just stayed."

In fact, he and some friends had set up a trekking business in Tibet. For the next thirty years they'd organised and guided treks through the mountains and had been as high as 20,000 feet. He'd led over thirty month-long, two-hundred mile treks in Tibet and helped on many Everest expeditions. He'd retired the business when in his seventies, because, as he said, "My joints are plumb worn out, I've had hip replacements and knee ops, can't do the long treks no more."

We stopped at the viewpoint overlooking the houses of Lower Voe and I thought I'd surprise him with Shetland's connection to Mount Everest. I told him that down by the shore at Lower Voe was where the firm of T.M. Adie & Sons had their knitwear factory. I went on to explain that John Hunt, leader of the first ascent of Everest in 1953, had placed a special order with the firm to produce a range of lightweight, woollen garments, specially made for each member of that expedition. Sir Edmund Hillary and Sherpa Tensing Norgay were wearing Shetland wool jumpers, scarves and socks when they conquered the mountain. These garments made near sea level had reached the highest point on Earth.

"Well I'll be jiggered!" he said, "I thought I knew most things about Everest but I sure didn't know that."

He wanted a photo of Lower Voe but had no camera with him so we later bought a postcard with a view of the village.

As we drove north I passed a comment that I knew that his hometown of Carmel was where Clint Eastwood was mayor. He replied that Eastwood's famous Mission Ranch was just across from his house. But I got the distinct impression he wasn't overly enamoured by his famous neighbour. From somewhere I also remembered that Carmel had been the home of author John Steinbeck, and I passed comment on this.

"Knew him," he said.

"What?" I said. "You knew Steinbeck?"

"Yep, when I was small boy he used to come 'round and get drunk with my uncle. Nice guy, mostly drunk. Used to sit on his knee, listened to him telling great yarns."

At lunchtime we stopped at Braewick Cafe and while waiting for our order Scotty began to write on the postcard of Lower Voe. I asked if he was sending it home.

"Nope," he said, "I'm sending this to my buddy Ed."

The penny was beginning to drop. "Ed?" I asked.

"Yeah, Ed Hillary, great buddy of mine. I'm telling him that I've just seen the village where his underwear was made."

Scotty went on to explain that along with Sir Edmund Hillary and others he'd help set up The American Himalayan Foundation of which he was still a board member. They build schools and hospitals for the children in Nepal, also supported the Dalai Lama in helping the expelled refugees from Tibet to settle in Nepal and India.

At some point I'd asked him why he'd come to Shetland and got a "Because it's there" sort of answer. Before coming to Shetland he'd hired a car and driven around Wales, sleeping in the car each night. I said to him that after that he'd be glad to be in the Lerwick guest house at night. But no, he told me that after thirty years of living mostly under canvas he hated walls; even now he never slept in a bed, always on a mat on the floor. Even in the short time I was in his company he was imparting his love for the mountains and culture of Tibet. I did get the impression that he was restless in his retirement from the Himalaya. I found out later that Scotty is a well respected friend to many mountaineers and Sherpas.

Sherpa Tensing Norgay and Sir Edmund Hillary wearing a Shetland wool jumper. Photo © Shetland Museum.

A couple of years later an American family consisting of a mother with her son, daughter and daughter-in-law, booked a North Mainland tour with me. We stopped at the Lower Voe viewpoint and I explained the Everest connection. I also commented that I'd recently done a tour with a Californian called Scotty Macbeth from the 1963 expedition. It came as a complete surprise when the mother said that her late husband had been a support climber on that famous expedition. I found out later that he was Barry Corbet, geologist and remarkable mountaineer, whose selfless efforts had made the first ever ascent of Everest's West Ridge possible. It is indeed a small world.

Do mention the war

Shetland and Shetlanders have been involved in all major world conflicts and these form a great part of our human history, from Viking times right through to the present. Visitors to Shetland are interested in this part of our heritage, especially our involvement in the two world wars of the 20th century. As a tour guide I had to bear in mind that some older guests may have had a direct connection with World War 2 and a little bit of discretion may be in order. Sometimes, though, it didn't work out just like that. Two German girl students from Hamburg had booked a tour of West Mainland. We'd stopped for lunch at the Friday pop-up cafe in the Waas Methodist Church. In conversation one of the girls commented on how nice the stained glass windows in the church looked. Not for the first time my tongue got ahead of my brain by about a couple of seconds when I said, "You'll have some nice stained glass windows in Hamburg too."

"No," one girl replied, as they both laughed at my immediate embarrassment, "you got rid of them all."

It was sometimes difficult to gauge the age of a person; some of my guests were about eighty but looked not much over sixty. One was Dick, a retired professor of English from New York. I'd asked him what his job was. "I've been ten years a merchant seaman and ten years a gravedigger to pay my way through college. I was twenty years a teacher, now I'm a boat-builder."

With his interest in boats I took him to the Unst Boat Haven and his knowledge of boats and their construction was impressive. I asked him if he'd been to Shetland before. "No," he said, "but I was somewhere north of here on my twenty-first birthday on my way to Murmansk."

He'd been a merchant seaman on convoys to Russia during the war.

Another time I had a small group in the Tangwick Haa museum and let the group wander but was on hand to answer any questions. Part of the display was a Morse key, so for old times' sake I idly tapped out CQ, CQ, CQ (meaning attention), then my name and Tangwick Haa in Morse, not thinking that anyone would be listening. I hadn't noticed the rather sprightly but quite elderly English lady standing behind me until she repeated back the words I'd tapped out. She explained that she'd lived in Germany before the war and was a fluent German speaker. At the outbreak of war she'd been recruited to work as a radio operator in the south of England, although she wouldn't specify exactly where. From our conversation it wasn't too difficult to work out that she had been an intercept radio operator for Bletchley Park.

My oldest guest ever was a bluff Yorkshire gentleman who twice booked tours with me in successive years at the ages of ninety and ninety-one. Due to a disability he'd been in the Home Guard during the war. After the war he'd become an expert on crop diseases and crop production in Africa and had travelled extensively through that continent. The first year he came on a tour he was still a working professor at a university in northern Nigeria, which also seemed to be his home. On his second visit to Shetland he said that he'd been told that it wouldn't be safe to go back as he would be an easy target for Boko Haram terrorists.

Probably the most poignant experience I had with a guest was on a tour of South Mainland. This gentleman was in his eighties and after collecting a few others from the Tourist Centre I picked him up from a guest house on the outskirts of Lerwick. He told me that he was originally from Edinburgh but now lived in France. He was a widower, and from what he said about his health I guessed this was probably the last time he would be able to tour around Scotland. At the end of the tour, after I'd dropped the others off, I was making arrangements to pick him up the next day. During the tour I'd noticed that he had no camera with him, so I commented on this and offered him the use of a spare digital one I carried for such an eventuality. He thanked me but said no, and remarked that he'd taken far too many photos in his life and would never take any more. Curious, I asked if he'd been a professional photographer, thinking that perhaps he'd been a film-only man. Then he told me his story.

During World War 2 he'd been called up to the RAF and had become a navigator on Lancaster bombers. From that he'd been transferred to a Mosquito reconnaissance and pathfinder squadron as a navigator and camera operator. Before the bombing raids on the German city of Dresden he'd taken the pre-raid reconnaissance photos and later had flown on a pathfinder mission on one of the raids. Following the raids he'd flown a photo-reconnaissance mission to survey the destruction of the city. He said that after he saw what had happened to Dresden that was the last time he'd touched a camera. He'd never been able to bring himself to take a photograph since. I can't say for certain, but I got the feeling that he'd never told this story before; maybe he felt that was the right time or the right opportunity.

There was a coincidental postscript to his story. The following week I was guiding two sisters from what was once Czechoslovakia, now living in England. They were very chatty, asking me about everything, including what Shetland did in the war. When they said they originally came from a small town near the German border I asked if it was far from Dresden. The eldest sister replied that it wasn't far and when she was about twelve years old she had helped her mother with a soup kitchen for the refugees fleeing from the Dresden bombing.

Shetland's role in wartime opposition to Nazi-occupied Norway through the clandestine operations from Lunna and Scalloway is of great interest to Norwegian visitors. Young Norwegians used fishing boats to land agents, weapons and supplies into occupied Norway and evacuate refugees. The Shetland Bus was the nickname of the special operations group that carried out these activities between 1941 and 1945. The memorial in Scalloway to the men who died on these operations is visited by many Norwegians, as is Scalloway Museum, where the story of these heroes is told. On one occasion I had two elderly sisters on a tour that included Scalloway. We'd stopped at the memorial and I noticed that both were a bit emotional so I asked if they'd visited Scalloway before. The youngest sister said yes she had, but couldn't remember the event because she was only two years old. They explained that they now lived in London but were Norwegian. The younger sister had been one of the refugees that had been smuggled out of Norway to Scalloway on one of the Shetland Bus boats after the invasion.

Shetland Bus memorial in Scalloway.

One Sunday morning in my first year of tour guiding, when I was still feeling my way a bit, I had a call from the Tourist Centre. They asked if I could come to the

Centre and take a Norwegian family of four out on a tour. The family consisted of an elderly couple with their daughter and son-in-law. The elderly gentleman of about eighty spoke excellent English, with a hint of a Scottish accent. We agreed on a tour of West Mainland as he was particularly interested in sheep and hill farming. I didn't think it unusual at first, but he was the only one who spoke English and interpreted all that I said to his family. Our first stop on the tour was Scalloway and the Shetland Bus memorial. I was a bit surprised that they hadn't heard of the Shetland Bus operation or of its most decorated captain, Shetland's Larsen. However, the elderly gentleman was quite interested as I explained all about the Shetland Bus and he interpreted for his family.

By now I was beginning to wonder why the younger members of the family didn't speak English, it being the second language in Norway. As I listened more carefully to the interpretation I came to the conclusion that he wasn't speaking Norwegian, in fact it sounded suspiciously like German. I suppose there was a fairly obvious pause in my speech while realisation began to dawn that perhaps I was explaining the heroic story of the Shetland Bus to a German of active World War 2 age. Hoping that the Tourist Centre hadn't got it wrong, and thinking perhaps they were from the far east of Norway, I asked, "What part of Norway did you say you were from?"

He obviously could see from my expression what I was thinking and clapped me on the shoulder. "Ha, my friend," he said, "we are not from Norway, we are from Austria."

At this point I should have remembered the First Law of Holes, which states that "When you find yourself in a hole, stop digging."

Feeling slightly relieved that he wasn't technically German, I remarked, "Your English is very good, were you an English teacher?"

He laughed. "No, my friend, I was three years prisoner of war in Scotland, there I learned my Scottish English."

He went on to tell me about himself. He was a sheep farmer from the Austrian Tyrol. At seventeen he'd been conscripted into the German army and had been sent to the Russian front. He said he had been one of the lucky ones as he'd been wounded and airlifted back to Germany. After recovering from his wounds he'd been posted to the Atlantic Wall defences and had surrendered to the British on D-Day. For most of his time as a prisoner of war he'd been billeted with a family on a farm in Perthshire, from where he worked in forestry. "You know," he said, "in three months we cut down more trees than the Italians did in three years!"

Following his repatriation he remained in contact with the family and visited them every time he came to Scotland.

Fine dining

Driving through Lerwick's streets at the start of a tour, almost always the first comment I'd hear was: "Every house seems to have a net hanging on the garden wall, are these fishermen drying their nets?"

Tempting as it was to make up a story, I would explain that these nets are supplied to households by Shetland Island Council to cover rubbish sacks on collection morning to protect them from marauding 'maas' and scavenging 'skories'.

On returning to Lerwick at the end of the day I'd almost always be asked: "Where are your fish restaurants?"

Then I have to explain that although Shetland is in the middle of the richest fishing grounds in Europe, and a great variety of fish is landed here, there are no dedicated fish restaurants to reflect this. Hotel restaurants rarely have more than one or two choices of fish and these rarely vary. I once had the pleasure of showing one of Italy's top tour guides for a premier tour company around Shetland. She loved Shetland but could not understand the lack of local produce, especially fish, on offer.

Of course Lerwick has no lack of Oriental and Asian dining establishments, similar to those most tourists can experience in their own home towns. In April one year two lads from India booked a South Mainland and a North Mainland tour with me. On booking they stated that they wanted to see puffins, whales, seals and otters. I explained that seals were easy to find but it was maybe a bit early for puffins, and sightings of whales and otters were down to the luck of being in the right place at the right time. On the South tour we saw seals on the shore outside Tesco, orcas in Mousa Sound, and were at Sumburgh Head when the puffins arrived. The next day we had a close view of a dog otter making his way along the ebb at Olna. The only downside of their visit was the curry they had at our first lunch stop at a hotel cafe-bar. It was too hot for them they said; they wouldn't have a curry that hot back home.

A couple and their daughter that I had on tour for a few days had an experience that could almost have come from a *Fawlty Towers* TV sketch. As we'd all be lunching together, the parents told me that their teenage daughter was recovering from an eating disorder; they were telling me this in advance because she was a very slow eater. As part of her recovery programme she had to eat at the table with us so they could make sure she was eating. They were really pleased with her progress and she now was choosing her own food from the menus. This worked well for our first day and I dropped them off at their hotel assuring them that they wouldn't have a problem with their evening meal there.

The next morning they told me what had happened. They'd decided to dine in their hotel and they'd all ordered from the menu; their daughter had ordered fish. After a while a flustered waiter came back to say that the fish she'd ordered was off but she could have a salt cod dish. The parents' order came but they'd nearly finished before the daughter's salt cod order eventually appeared. Her father described her fish dish to me as something resembling a charred slab of off-white cardboard drowned in a white sauce. He reckoned it was practically inedible to anyone with a healthy appetite far less anyone trying to overcome an eating disorder. He was worried that this experience would be a huge setback, but fortunately his daughter hadn't batted an eyelid and just worked her way around the inedible fish. We could only assume that whoever was in the kitchen had no idea that salt cod had to be re-hydrated by soaking for hours in water and then boiled or baked. They'd obviously taken the hard, dry slab of salt cod and tried to fry or grill it.

In my first year of operating my business I would stop at a viewpoint looking south across the broad sweep of St Magnus Bay and a magnificent view of Brae Wick with the iconic Drongs sea-stacks in the foreground. One day when I stopped there I found a building site. Thinking that one of the best views in Shetland would be blocked from the road, I made enquiries. I needn't have worried; the site was to become a much needed cafe, caravan park and campsite. The following year the Braewick Cafe had opened and I could wow my customers with the view while they enjoyed the good food and hospitality of Christina and her husband, Magnus. They were kind enough to incorporate displays from Geopark Shetland on the site and provide access to Shetland's most spectacular shingle beach. A visit to the cafe with its outstanding panorama became an integral part of my twice-weekly North Mainland tours; a stop that all my guests enjoyed enormously. Here my guests would find the most helpful staff and it was always service with a smile, especially from Aurore, who would always bring a ray of sunshine, even to the dullest and wettest days.

Shetland does pretty well for cafes, most being in and around Lerwick and Scalloway, but more are opening further afield as Shetland's tourism industry continues to grow. Brae has Frankie's – Britain's most northerly fish and chip shop – and on the same street, the most northerly Indian takeaway. Some cafes are in visitor centres such as the excellent Hoswick Visitor Centre in Hoswick. Others, such as Tangwick Haa Museum, Quendale Mill or Scalloway Museum are self-service, where you can make a cup of tea or coffee and purchase a biscuit or a homebake. Each Sunday during the summer there are always a few village halls serving fundraising "Sunday Teas" that are popular with locals and visitors alike.

I would run weekly tours to Unst and for a lunch break we'd stop at The Final Checkout supermarket in Baltasound that has an excellent cafe attached. It takes its name on account of it being the most northerly supermarket in the British Isles. On seeing the sign for the first time I had a guest who suggested The Final Checkout would be a good name for undertakers. Another time I had an American couple on tour who thought that Shetland mussels couldn't possibly be as nice as the ones from near their home island off the Washington coast. A visit to the Pierhead bar and restaurant at Voe proved them wrong.

Probably the all-time great dining experience for my guests occurred at the Crofthouse Museum with Ian a' Trossick, the crofter-cum-curator extraordinaire. On one occasion I visited there with a group of four guests to find Ian grilling freshly caught mackerel fillets over a glowing peat fire. He invited us all to help ourselves, which we did; no knives forks or plates, just fingers. They all agreed that this was just the best dining experience they'd ever had.

Fit the Tenth: Hamefarin

Our ancestors are totally essential to our every waking moment, although most of us don't even have the faintest idea about their lives, their trials, their hardships or challenges. (Annie Lennox.)

Shetland, our Auld Rock, seems to have a magnetic attraction that is passed down through the genes. Over the years I've toured with quite a number of descendants of Shetlanders who had left our shores for various corners of the New World during the 19th and 20th centuries. On many occasions I've been able to assist those who have wanted to find out more details of the land where their ancestors lived and left. I've taken some to the very croft or crofting township they knew only as a name on a census form. Sometimes I've even been able to help solve historical family puzzles going back generations.

Redders of the lost kin

One morning I'd picked up a lady and her husband from the ferry terminal for a South Mainland tour. "Do we go anywhere near a place called Boddam?" she asked. I replied that the tour would take us through the settlement of Boddam on our way to the Crofthouse Museum. She went on to say that her grandfather had been a doctor in Boddam and her father had been born there. She said that if possible she'd like to see the house. I said that I didn't know exactly where that would be, but I knew a man who did and we'd be meeting him later.

That man was of course Ian a' Trossick at the Crofthouse Museum. We entered the Crofthouse by stooping through low doorways. Opening the low but-end door was a portal back in time to a vision any Shetland emigrant in the last two hundred years could have called home. Ian was ensconced in a straight-backed wooden chair by a 'lowin' paet fire, Friday's *Shetland Times* open on his lap. Sunbeams streaming through the window lit up gently swirling horizontal layers of blue paet smoke that filled the but-end above his head. A crofter in timeless repose after a hard morning's work. As always, Ian made visitors feel at home and at ease. He could tell my guest that the doctor's house had been demolished but the site and the garden wall was still there. This was not far from the Crofthouse so we went along for my guests to take photos of the site. Ian also told us that he had photographs of the house before demolition, so I arranged to copy these and post them on to my delighted guest.

The doctor's house in Boddam, now demolished. Photo © Ian Smith.

It was mostly poverty and hopes of a better life that drove thousands of Shetlanders from our shores. Although one lady from New Zealand had a slightly different take on it. Her ancestors had come from Papa Stour, so I took her over to the island where we hiked almost a complete island circuit following the coast. It had started a nice sunny, breezy day with Papa looking at its best. From the top of the Hill of Feilie the old crofting toonships in the east wore their summer mantle of green in dramatic contrast to the moorland and rugged coastline to the west. My guest was impressed: "I can't believe that my ancestors would wish to leave such a beautiful island."

A few quick, light showers came on in the early afternoon but even without waterproofs these caused us no problem. An ominously dark cloud was building up over Ronas Hill to the north and by late afternoon a seriously heavy shower came down on us. We were crossing open moorland but managed to cower beside a large boulder that afforded no more than token shelter. Summer became winter in an instant; the wind howled as a squall line swept over us in a welter of rain, sleet and hail just to complete our soaking. "Now I know why my ancestors left the island!"

Papa Stour looking towards Ronas Hill.

Poor weather and chance helped solve a family mystery for another lady, this time from Australia. I'd gone to the Tourist Centre to collect a couple of guests to find another five passengers waiting to join my tour. Their boat trip from Lerwick around Bressay had been cancelled due to strong winds so my scenery and archaeology tour of South Mainland seemed the best alternative.

We'd had a good day and, as sometimes happens, my guests would take turns to sit in the front seats for a better view. Driving back at the end of the tour the lady sitting up front asked if I'd heard of a place called Hamar, or somewhere called North Lees. I said that I knew of an abandoned croft called North Lees on the north shore of Hamar Voe in North Mainland, if that was the one she meant.

She didn't know if that was it for sure, but asked if I could possibly take her there, then went on to explain that her grandfather, who she could remember, had most likely come from Shetland. Her mother had found letters after his death sent from a sister from North Lees and later one from a place called Innabanks. All they knew was that her grandfather had been on a ship in a German port at the start of World War 1 and had been interned for the duration of the war. After they'd been released from the internment camp he'd found a ship heading for Australia where he'd met her grandmother and settled down.

The woman had been in Scotland on business and had come to Shetland on the off-chance of finding some information on her grandfather. The next day I drove her to the road end at Olnesfirth in North Mainland from where an old track leads down to the shore and the deserted croft of North Lees. I knew its locality because several years earlier I'd been on a walk to the old 19th century herring fishing station near there. We started to walk down the old track then, acting just on a pure hunch, I retraced my steps and went up to a modern croft house close by. I had no idea who lived there, but I thought that I would ask if they knew anything about the old croft. An elderly lady answered the door. I enquired about North Lees saying that the lady with me had the family name Nicholson and perhaps had a connection with the croft. We were immediately invited in to speak to her husband.

Her husband was Eddie, who I had met once before so he knew who I was. I explained our errand and my companion related the story of her grandfather and the possibility of a connection to North Lees. Eddie told us that he'd lived in the area all his life and when he was a small boy a man with a long white beard lived in that croft. He went on to say that this man had two of a family; a son and a daughter. The daughter had moved from North Lees to Innabanks. He'd never heard what happened to the son and no-one seemed to know what became of him. It soon became fairly obvious that the missing son in question was this lady's grandfather. By pure chance I'd taken her to the house of probably the only man in Shetland still alive who had known her great-grandfather and her great-aunt. Not only that but Eddie was very much into local genealogy and could put her in touch with cousins she never knew she had.

Eddie was delighted that we'd stopped by and accompanied us down to North Lees where he was able to tell my guest much of her family history and about their life on the croft. On the drive back to Lerwick she asked if I'd known all along that Eddie lived there and knew about the family. I said that I hadn't, and it was just luck that for no particular reason I'd decided to ask at the house. She remarked that fate must have taken a hand, for if her boat trip hadn't been cancelled she wouldn't have been on my tour, and if I hadn't acted on my hunch she would have never have found her family history.

I was able to surprise an Australian couple who arrived in Shetland with only a patchy knowledge of their Shetland ancestors. They were booked for three days of tours as part of a small group arriving from Orkney by ferry. This couple were waiting for me when I arrived so we had a chat while we waited for the others. They introduced themselves as Williamson; I remarked that Williamson was a common Shetland name. The husband then told me that he did indeed have a Shetland ancestry. He went on to say that his great-grandfather had been the first minister of the Congregational Church at a place called Sullom. He was delighted when I told him I knew where that church was, and since our tour of North Mainland the next day would pass close by Sullom, I would make a diversion to let him see the church. He also went on to say that he'd been told that he was distantly related to a Johnny "Notions" Williamson and to a Laurence Tulloch. I could tell from what he was saying that he knew very little about the history of those two names and their significance in Shetland folklore. I decided that I wouldn't tell him about those men just then or that a visit to Johnny Notions' grave was on the itinerary for the next day, but would save it as a surprise.

The morning of the North tour was wet and misty with cloud well down on the hills; weather that obscured many of my viewpoints and made my job a bit more challenging. Because of the hill fog we'd miss some higher viewpoints but the others in the group were enthused by the prospect of a diversion to the great-grandfather's Church and to participate in redding-up of the Williamson kin. All were delighted with the Church visit and as the morning went on the weather improved considerably. Lunch at the Braewick Cafe was another highlight, then I sprung my surprise. I told them that after lunch we'd be visiting the grave of John Williamson aka "Johnny Notions", so called because he was a man of ideas. During the 18th and 19th centuries smallpox was the scourge of Shetland, but to combat this, Johnny Notions devised an effective method of inoculation which he practiced widely throughout Shetland. Johnny Notions is very much a local hero and lies in the well-tended graveyard of the ruined medieval Cross Kirk on Esha Ness.

Once we'd paid our respects to Johnny Notions I brought everyone over to the nearby grave of one Donald Robertson. His tabular gravestone bears this remarkable legend: *Donald Robertson, born 14th January 1785, died 4th June 1848, aged 63 years. He was a peaceable, quiet man and to all appearance a sincere Christian.*

His death was much regretted, which was caused by the stupidity of Laurence Tulloch in Clothister (Sullom) who sold him nitre instead of Epsom salts by which he was killed in the space of 5 hours after taking a dose of it.

The evening before, I'd done a bit of research and discovered that Laurence Tulloch was in fact the father-in-law of the Reverend Laurence Williamson, the great-grandfather of my guest. So Laurence Tulloch, infamous for dispensing a lethal dose of nitre (potassium nitrate), was his great-great-grandfather. A sad tale, but nevertheless such successful redding of lost kin was one of the great pleasures of tour-guiding.

On one occasion it was my own kin that, to my surprise, got a bit reddit. A young lady from Canada had booked a South Mainland tour with me, prior to hiring a car and exploring West Mainland where some of her ancestors came from in the early 1900s. She had the name of the township and of the croft so it was easy for me to pinpoint it on the map for her.

Just in conversation I asked her how far back in Shetland she had traced her ancestors. "As far back as a Peter Fraser from Walls in about 1740," she replied.

That came as a surprise, for on my father's side of the family I trace the Frasers back to a Peter Fraser about 1740. A follow-up online at the amazing Bayanne House family history website showed that we were indeed both descendants of the same Peter Fraser; I from his first marriage and she from his second.

Her Shetland ancestors had left for Canada in the early 1900s. The other side of her family, her Liverpool ancestors, had gone to Canada about the same time. We drove through Scalloway and passed the Walter and Joan Gray Eventide Home, named after the benefactors of the home. I pointed out a Canada connection by saying that this Scalloway couple had emigrated then married and settled in Canada. Following Walter's career with Marconi and a spell of retirement in Canada they'd returned to Scalloway to live. I also mentioned that Walter Gray had been the radio operator at Cape Race Lighthouse and it was he that had received the distress call from *RMS Titanic*. She then told me that she was indeed fortunate to be here as her Liverpool ancestors had been due to sail on the *Titanic*. The husband of the family had bought tickets for the voyage but when he got home his wife had thought them too expensive and made him change them for another ship. The other ship they sailed on was *RMS Carpathia*, the ship that picked up survivors from *Titanic*.

A couple from England were having a one day tour on Shetland, having arrived in the morning by ferry from Orkney and were leaving the same evening by ferry to Aberdeen. The tour was to be to Mousa but the ferry to the island had been cancelled due to strong winds. As a substitute tour we were doing Clickimin broch, Scalloway and West Mainland. Not long into the tour they asked me if I knew the name Isbister. I said that I did; it is the name of a place, also a family name. They said they'd never been to Shetland before but some years back had owned a smallholding on which they bred Shetland cattle. The pedigree stock they'd used came from Shetland with the name of Isbister. We were just leaving Scalloway as they told me this so without saying anything much I drove across the bridge to the island of Trondra and down to the Burland croft. Just outside the byre I saw Mary Isbister from whose pedigree stock their cattle had come. To the surprise of my guests I introduced them to Mary in less than ten minutes from them asking me if I knew the name. It was not just people whose kin I could red up, I could do kye as well.

Group on the Croft Trail, Burland, Trondra.

Media moments

My three minutes of prime-time TV fame came by chance. Someone at the Open University had my phone number and passed it on to the researcher for the second series of BBC TV's *Coast* programme. She and the producer were coming to Shetland to research part of a programme on Shetland and Orkney and had heard about a tsunami that had swept across Shetland over seven thousand years ago. They wanted to see if there was anywhere they could film evidence of this and if I could tell them about it. As it happened I knew where the best exposure of the tsunami evidence was and I knew a geomorphologist, Adrian Hall, who had dating evidence of the tsunami so I put her in touch with him. A bit later she contacted me again, Adrian had agreed to take part in the filming so would I show her and producer the locality to check out its suitability. They duly arrived in Shetland and we hired a RIB boat in the evening to take us to the locality on the west shore of Sullom Voe – a place called Maggie Kettle's Loch. This all went well and they were happy with the locality and that Adrian could come to Shetland to film with them in a few weeks time.

On the way back they asked me if I knew of anywhere else in Shetland that might be of interest for the programme and I suggested the volcanic coast of Esha Ness along to the amazing storm beach at the Grind o' da Navir. The Grind is a breach in the cliffs inside which storm waves have torn a vast amphitheatre by splitting off great slabs of bedrock weighing several tons and piling them up inland. This is one of the most spectacular features of the British coastline and the *Coast* team were most impressed. Not least as by time we got there it was well after 10pm on a calm summer's evening. The setting sun was shining through the Grind, bathing the massive beach ridge of boulders in an orange glow. They decided then and there to include Esha Ness in the programme when I pointed out that Adrian, who was doing the tsunami with them, had co-authored a scientific paper on the Grind. There my involvement with the programme ended, or so I thought.

A few weeks later I got a call on my mobile while I was dropping off guests at Sumburgh airport. This was the *Coast* producer. They'd done all the tsunami filming but unfortunately Adrian wouldn't have time to film at the Grind o' da

Grind o' da Navir, Esha Ness.

Navir. He'd suggested that I could do it just as well as him. I explained that I was eighty miles away by road but if they were happy to wait I would join them at Esha Ness Lighthouse. There I met the filming team and presenter Nick Crane, just five of them, no big production budget this.

It was an education to see how filming part of such an excellent programme as *Coast* is done. No fuss, just professionalism all the way through. Nick Crane, an experienced explorer, author and presenter, rather surprisingly seemed a shy person at first, but became more talkative as we walked along the coast to the Grind and the storm beach. When we got there, there was no storyboard or script. I was wired with a radio mic and Nick and I walked through the storm beach to the Grind, just chatting about the place and how it formed, as we were filmed. When we'd finished the camera operator explained that for something like this they'd use three cameras to film us simultaneously from different positions. They only had one camera so it had to be repositioned and we had to repeat the same walk and talk at least three times.

I think we did it about five times before the producer was happy. After three takes I'd forgotten much of the order I'd explained things in the first, but apparently that didn't matter as they'd use the audio from the first take. At the end, when the producer was happy, everybody apart from Nick sat down on rocks and relaxed. The whole process of filming my three minutes on prime time TV had taken over two hours. Nick then wandered off, he paced up and down for about five minutes talking to himself, but nobody seemed perturbed at this. When Nick came back I handed him his trademark rucksack with the umbrella attached. Everyone got up and they recorded his final summary piece to camera; this he did straight off, no script and no retakes. Here I can reveal one of television's best kept secrets: the iconic rucksack with the umbrella, used in all his documentaries, is just a padded-out prop for filming.

This was the first time I'd been filmed for a TV programme, although I had been consulted some years before by the producer and presenter of a Landscape Mysteries TV programme called *The Tower People of Shetland*. This series was presented by the remarkable professor Aubrey Manning, who had also fronted the fascinating BBC2 *Earth Story* series. Over a beer in the Grand Hotel he quizzed me on the geology of Shetland. Although they were primarily making an archaeological programme about Iron Age brochs, the ever thorough Manning wanted to know as much as he could about how Shetland's landscape formed. He wanted to understand as much as possible how the Iron Age people would adapt and fit into Shetland's landscape and environment.

A couple of years later I was at a European Geoparks conference as part of Shetland's bid acquire Geopark status when I felt a tap on my shoulder. It was Aubrey Manning. Although we had only met once before he'd recognised me. He was very supportive of our Geopark bid after his Shetland experience. Another programme I helped out with was *Making Scotland's Landscape*, written and presented by geologist professor Iain Stewart. Much of this was also filmed at the Grind o' da Navir.

Professor Ian Stewart surveys the cliff-top storm beach at the Grind o' da Navir.

November in Shetland is well outside our tourist season so I was surprised to be asked to take around crew from a French national television channel, TF1. They had come to Shetland to make a mini-documentary on the islands to include in their rolling news programme over Christmas. They were lucky with the weather as both filming days were dry and reasonably calm. Shetland in November sometimes isn't conducive to filming landscape. The freelance cameraman had been in Shetland before, filming the wreck of the oil tanker *Braer* in January 1993, so he'd come dressed for all eventualities of the weather, but the others really weren't. The main focus of the documentary was to be on wool production and knitting, in effect they wanted the whole process from "ewe to you". The programme was to include an interview they'd set up with Hazel Tindall, the world's fastest knitter, and a visit to the Sandness spinning mill. They also wanted shots of the variety of natural-coloured wool found on native Shetland sheep. This was going to be quite a challenge for me in November.

The first day filming with the TF1 team was a cloudy, windless day with good visibility. To combine scenery with the best chance of encountering coloured Shetland hill sheep I decided to take them around Northmavine, with a drive up Collafirth Hill for the best all-round view of the landscape. We'd seen little in the way of sheep on the way to Ollaberry, but out of the corner of my eye I'd noticed some stock trailers and pick-ups parked up a track near some empty sheep pens. They were still there on the way back so I devised a cunning plan. I realised that the vehicle owners must be gathering hill sheep somewhere close to bring them to the pens in order to separate the breeding ewes from the flock. I parked near the pens and instructed the cameraman to set up on a small rise overlooking the track, telling him that a flock of sheep would shortly be passing there.

After five minutes: "C'est impossible, no sheeps here." I told them not to worry as I was sure that they would come. Five minutes later: "C'est magnifique!" as a large multicoloured 'caa', driven by crofters and their dogs, passed right below the camera towards the pens. Not only did they get their sheep footage but interviews with local crofters as well. The next day was bright and breezy so

I planned to take them to St Ninian's Isle, but first we'd visit Shetland Museum in Lerwick to film some footage inside. There was just one other visitor in the museum, who turned out to be a French lady. She agreed to come to St Ninian's Isle with us to be filmed walking on the sand tombolo and to be interviewed about her visit to Shetland in her own language. She was probably the only French tourist in the whole of Shetland in November and a very timely chance meeting for the film crew.

Most winter tourists come for Lerwick's Up-Helly-A' fire festival on the last Tuesday in January. Perhaps surprisingly, on average, the weather in Up-Helly-A' week can be reasonably benign. Over the years Lerwick Up-Helly-A' has grown from a small, relaxed local festival to become a large, regimented tourism spectacular that attracts visitors and film crews from all over the world. Most of my tours on that week involved film crews getting some background footage and filming the festival itself.

One year I had a film crew of just two from Brazil: a father and son-in-law team, Mauricio and Laurencio, making a documentary about Shetland and the festival. We filmed background material at Jarlshof on the day they arrived and in North Mainland the next day. On Up-Helly-A' day we filmed activities in and around the town and of course the procession and longship-burning in the evening. I'd even managed to obtain them tickets for Bell's Brae hall to see some of guizers performing in there.

During the day we'd shot some footage in Clickimin broch, where I happened to be wearing my rather old and battered waxed, canvas hat. Mauricio asked if I minded if they filmed me inside the broch telling them all about the archaeology. I said I was fine with that, so we went ahead and all went well with my piece to camera.

When we'd finished I asked Mauricio what company they were making the film for.

"Globo TV, the second largest channel in the world. This will be part of a two-hour Sunday afternoon programme in Brazil; there will be over ninety million viewers." Then, indicating my hat: "We are going to introduce you as Shetland's Indiana Jones!"

Laurencio looked at me: "Ha, you look more like his father in that hat".

Certainly the first and last time that I've ever been likened to Sean Connery.

Television was not the only media that I guided for. On the 4th and 5th of January, when Shetland was still in the collective re-entry phase from Yule and New Year excesses, I had the pleasure of introducing the Digital Nomad to Shetland. *National Geographic Traveller* Andrew Evans was a new breed of travel writer, tweeting and interacting with his followers in real time (or as near as possible) as he went along. He was also blessed with good weather; the most difficult task was finding internet hotspots for him to communicate his photographic selfies and text to the world.

Print was another media that I sometimes guided for; some tours were for magazine travel writers and others were for book authors. The first original travel book on Shetland for about two hundred years was Ron McMillan's *Between Weathers; Travels in 21st Century Shetland*. I accompanied Ron on some of his travels around Mainland. A few years later I guided New Zealand author Jean Bennett, who writes for *National Geographic Learning*: *Kids Around The World* series. Following her visit to Shetland she wrote *Stormy Seas: A Story from the Shetland Islands. Four young friends learn about their Shetland Islands Heritage.* Much of our conversations on her visit were about my childhood and growing up in Shetland. It was Jean who first suggested that I should write about growing up and my life in Shetland. This is that book, if you've stuck with my ramblings this far I hope you've enjoyed it.

Tailpiece

Tour guiding was certainly the most rewarding job I've done, not financially, but certainly the most enjoyable. Once I'd started guiding I very soon came to realise that being a tour guide is not simply about driving people around, imparting information by rote and answering questions. First and foremost a guide is an ambassador for Shetland; your customers are your guests and they are Shetland's guests, so you must treat them as such. If, at the end of your time with them, they've enjoyed their tours and enjoyed Shetland then they will tell others when they get home.

I would always tell my guests at the end of their stay to come back and see the rest of Shetland. Many did. Not long after I started the business Janet and Francis, two ladies from London, booked a tour with me on their first visit to Shetland and have been coming back every year since. If you have achieved that sort of response then you will feel you have done your job. That *is* job satisfaction.

I never planned to be a tour guide, but then I never planned to be a geologist or a meteorologist or a fishworker or a radio operator.

Did I find my "proper job?" Maybe my search was akin to Lewis Carroll's *The Hunting of the Snark*. I could have titled this book *The Hunting of the 'Wark'*. Perhaps the question should be "Did I do a proper job in showcasing Shetland?" That is for others to answer. At least some of my guests thought so judging by their comments on TripAdvisor (*see Excursus 4*) and that's good enough for me.

Excursus 1:
A Lady of Comfort and Kindness –
Ellen (Nellie) Deans Allan

The 21st day of July 1881 was the blackest in the history of North Yell. A violent storm had overwhelmed many of the sixaereens out at sea at the haaf fishing the night before. When the storm had passed ten boats had gone; fifty-eight fishermen were drowned leaving thirty-four widows and eighty-five fatherless bairns. Only seven bodies were given up by the sea for burial. Thirty-six of the fishermen came from the communities around Gloup in North Yell. Not a single household in North Yell was unaffected by this most awful disaster. The future for so many must have seemed bleak indeed, with breadwinners gone, no safety net of state support and the roof over the heads of widows and orphans dependent solely on the whim of often unsympathetic landlords.

Even the blackest of clouds is said to have a silver lining and this for many came in the form of a most remarkable lady, Ellen Deans Allan (née Smith). Known as Nellie, she was the wife of the Free Church minister, the Reverend James Hamilton Allan. They'd arrived in Sellafirth from Aberdeenshire to take up the ministry of North Yell during the winter prior to his induction to the parish in January 1881. With hardly any time to get to know their parishioners and their customs, to minister the aftermath of the Gloup disaster must have been an onerous task for them. It seems that it was Nellie, more so than her husband, that rose to the challenge. She visited every bereaved family, giving as much comfort and practical support as she could, by all accounts above and beyond the call of duty of a minister's wife.

I was given the Christian name Allen after my maternal grandmother, Ellen Deans Allan Nisbet (who was also known as Nellie). My grandmother was born in Cunnister (near Sellafirth) in November 1881, in a community still suffering from the shock of the Gloup disaster. She was baptised Ellen Deans Allan Nisbet by the Reverend Allan. The family story is that she was named after Nellie Allan, who had offered to adopt her.

Author's grandmother Ellen (Nellie) Deans Allan Nisbet.

Nellie Allan was always fondly remembered in conversation by our family, although only my grandfather and grandmother would have been old enough to have known her well. I was too young to remember much detail of this; my grandmother died when I was four years old and my grandfather when I was nine. After the Gloup disaster Nellie continued to work to improve the lot of the people of North Yell, and Sellafirth in particular. This is her story:

Ellen (Nellie) Deans Smith was very much a daughter of the Manse. She was born on 21st April, 1851, at Keig (near Alford) Aberdeenshire, fifth of eleven children to the Free Church minister Reverend William Pirie Smith and Jane Robertson. Nellie and her siblings had a happy and lively upbringing although the household routines and education were very structured along religious lines. The rural setting of the Manse at Keig gave the children access to the countryside and introduced them to gardening, keeping pets and even a little crofting when they kept hens and a Shetland cow for milk. Her father ministered to a rural farming area of Keig and Tough, but the family also had connections with the sea and the coastal villages of Aberdeenshire, so Nellie would be familiar with life on both. Her father is described as being *"an accomplished scholar, a trained and skilful teacher, a theologian widely read, a preacher of singular penetration and power, yet he saw it his duty to devote himself altogether to the work of his congregation and the training of his family"*[1]. A description that in some respects could fit Nellie herself.

Nellie's mother Jane seems to have been a practical, down-to-earth person and the unobtrusive rock of the family and *"a woman of great force of character"*[2]. Being part of such a large family Nellie also knew and experienced tragedy. Deaths of a younger sister aged four and a newborn brother occurred when she was only six. Her eldest sibling, Mary Jane, nursed her older brothers William Robertson and George Michie who were afflicted by that scourge of 19th century Scotland, consumption (tuberculosis). When Nellie was thirteen, Mary Jane died from the disease. A year later George Michie succumbed, shortly after gaining a place at Cambridge to study mathematics. Seeing the way her mother coped with family illness and bereavements whilst bringing up a young family must have been a valuable lesson in preparing Nellie for the aftermath of the Gloup disaster.

Like the rest of her siblings Nellie was educated mostly at home, firstly by her mother Jane and, when far enough advanced, by her father. A former teacher and rector at Aberdeen's West End Academy, he'd been called to the Free Church after the Disruption of the Kirk in 1843. His teaching was to a high standard as he taught boarding-pupils at the manse to university level in order to supplement his stipend income. Bible study and family worship was a major component in the education of the Manse bairns, but languages and the latest scientific thinking played a part, especially with Reverend William and the older boys.

---

1   *William Robertson Smith: His Life, His Work and His Times*. Bernhard Maier.
2   Ibid.

Ellen (Nellie) Deans Smith in her twenties. Photo © Astrid Hess.

Nellie and her sisters were treated rather differently than the boys, following the 19th century educational belief that being female equated to being less able to achieve. Of Nellie her sister Alice wrote: *"Ellen was a lively, strong character and highly sociable; she loved music and art and became more proficient than any of the rest of us as both a pianist and amateur artist"*[3]. Elder brother William Robertson Smith survived the afflictions of TB and, like his late brother, was exceptionally gifted academically. He went on to a brilliant, and at times controversial, academic career as a professor of divinity, an acclaimed scholar and editor of *Encyclopaedia Britannica*. Overshadowed by brilliant elder brothers, and being a girl of the 19th century, Nellie's light was perhaps hidden under bushel; a parable that her family somewhat overlooked in her case.

Home education and being 'Manse bairns' kept Nellie and her siblings isolated from their peers in Keig. It was only when they went away to university (boys) and school (girls) in Aberdeen and Edinburgh that they mixed with children of their own age (and social class). Nellie accompanied William to Edinburgh while he was at university there from 1866 to 1870, and herself took lessons in French, drawing and music. At home after Edinburgh she honed her teaching skills on her younger siblings. In 1872 she again accompanied William on his study travels to further her education. This time it was to Göttingen in Germany where she stayed on after her brother returned to Scotland. A diphtheria epidemic swept Göttingen and Nellie was struck down by it. She recovered to meet, find romance, and then get engaged to a divinity student, only to meet the disapproval of both families. Eventually there was the heartbreak of an engagement that was stretched by enforced separation for three years in their respective home countries to the point where it broke off. Her sister Alice wrote: *"Her hair turned grey in that time and, though she remained the same kind, patient and loving sister she had always been, she grew very serious and completely lost her youthful vivacity"*[4].

On her enforced return to Scotland (whilst engaged) she undertook a variety of educational activities and teaching. Her excellent language skills and biblical knowledge were ably demonstrated in her 1874 translation of a theological work, Gustav Oehler's *Theology of the Old Testament*, from German to English. As well her excellent educational abilities Nellie was obviously a very capable person both practically and socially. Skills that didn't go unnoticed by the assistant to her father, the newly ordained Free Kirk minister James Hamilton Allan, who she married on 11th October, 1876.

James Hamilton Allan was born in Gallatown, Fife, in 1839, although he later claimed it was 1846, taking seven years off his age on his marriage certificate! He studied at Glasgow University and at the English Presbyterian Hall then was licensed by the Presbytery of London. Prior to his ministry training he was in business in Glasgow, but felt called to the work of the ministry and acted for a time as a missionary to a congregation in Manchester. He was then appointed

---

3   *Children of the Manse, Growing Up in Victorian Aberdeenshire.* Alice Thiele Smith, Astrid Hess, Gordon K. Booth.
4   Ibid.

U. F. CHURCH & MANSE,
KEIG & TOUGH.

*The Manse and Church in Keig, Aberdeenshire;
Nellie's family home. Photo © Astrid Hess.*

assistant to Nellie's father. James may not have lived entirely by the ethos expected of a man of the cloth, and a Free Kirk one at that. Not long after Nellie's engagement had ended her younger sisters Lucy and Alice were going to stay in Germany for a time to further their education. Shortly before Lucy's departure James, on bended knee, proposed to her in the Manse garden. Lucy had barely reached Germany when James proposed to Nellie! *"After Nellie's German engagement had ended so sadly, she in 1876 was wooed by her father's vicar, the Reverend James Hamilton Allan. He was a five years older theologian, of whom we know that he a short time before first had proposed her younger sister Lucy, which Nellie probably never got to know. All in all Nellie's husband must have been that kind of a man, who never was able to pass a pinafore without grabbing for the wearer"*[5].

The Reverend James Hamilton Allan and his new wife's first parish was at Glenbuchat, Strathdon, in Aberdeenshire. At Glenbuchat it seems that the Reverend Allan didn't live up to the expectations of his congregation, especially with his frequent absences to visit friends in Aberdeen. Whatever the problem was, be it business interests or an eye for the ladies, by 1880 the Reverend Allan's congregation had had enough and he was moved. The Allans arrived in Shetland during November 1880 and he was inducted into the Parish of North Yell and to Sellafirth Free Church on 12th January, 1881.

Sellafirth is situated on the east shore of the long inlet of Basta Voe, just one of five crofting communities around its shores, the other four are: Basta, Colvister, Dalsetter and Cunnister. The 1881 census shows Sellafirth having seventeen families, Basta fourteen, Colvister eight, Dalsetter seven and Cunnister twelve; 58 households in total. These were mostly large families of seven persons or more. It was a similar situation throughout the rest of North Yell.

Although both may have had knowledge of the farming and fishing communities of Aberdeenshire it can hardly have prepared them for North Yell in the early 1880s. Yell's gently rolling hills of heather covered peat, totally devoid of trees, would have seemed stark indeed, especially before they shed their brown winter coat. The standard of accommodation of crofters' houses would have been much more primitive than seen at home. Some would still be just one room with a fire in the centre of the floor and a hole in the roof for smoke. Turf and straw roofs would be the norm. Agricultural land was much poorer and farming practice at least fifty years behind what they had left. Diet was poor and monotonous.

Crofters were tenants, mostly tied to their landlord's haaf fishing in the summer months, leaving the women and children to do the croft work so families could subsist. At first the Shetland accent and dialect of Norse and Scots would have been almost as unintelligible as a foreign language. Not only that, they had arrived into a North Yell where communities were still in recovery from disruptions of the clearances ten to twelve years before. Many had been subjected to intimidation and eviction as whole crofting townships were cleared

---

5 Astrid Hess. Nellie's great-great niece (pers.comm.).

by the hated factor of the Garth Estate, John Walker. The Church had done little or nothing to oppose these evictions. Church ministers were seen to be in the same social class as the lairds and were supportive of their actions. Nellie was as far from home comforts and family as it was possible to be in Britain, transported to a world so different from settled, rural Aberdeenshire. In their first few weeks in Shetland Nellie must have wondered, Dear God, why us?

Compared to the crofters' hovels, the Sellafirth Manse the Allans moved into was from a different planet. Built in 1848, similar in style to the lairds' 'Haa' houses, it was an impressive, two-storey, slate-roofed building close to the church. Built at the same time as the Manse, the Free Church was designed to hold three-hundred souls at a service. Standing at the top of the Lee of Sellafirth to dominate the skyline, it was visible to all the crofting townships around Basta Voe. It was the crofters that had provided the labour to cart materials and build both the Church and the Manse. Shingle from the North Ayre of Cunnister was rowed by boats half the length of the voe and landed on the beach at the foot of the hill. Women carried the shingle up the steep Lee on their backs. There is a story that when the Manse was finally completed and everyone assembled to admire the result of their hard work, it was expected that a dram would be offered to all, as was the custom. No dram was forthcoming. One elderly lady, who had been involved in the carrying and was peeved by the lack of a dram, made this prediction: "Da Manse wis biggit dry, so it'll sit weet"[6]. True to her word the manse has been plagued by dampness ever since.

Manse and Church, Sellafirth, Yell; 1960s.

James Hamilton Allan is an enigma. Nellie's sister Alice had a low opinion of him: *"James Hamilton Allan turned out to be a weak, shiftless character, unsuited really to being a minister, and quite lacking any of Nellie's drive and initiative. They had no children and it was Nellie who ended up doing the lion's share of the pastoral work amongst the congregation there, holding classes for the children*

---

6   Told by my mother, Ann Fraser.

and becoming greatly admired by the local folk. She would even go up to the pulpit when Hamilton was unfit to do so"[7]. This is in stark contrast to his glowing obituary written by the Free Church[8].

When Nellie and her husband arrived in Sellafirth they found the Church and the Manse in poor condition: *"When Mr. Allan was settled at Sellafirth, the church and manse, which were much out of repair, were put in excellent order at considerable cost; and to his exertions also the mission hall at Seafield, Mid Yell, where he frequently held service, was well furnished"*[9]. In all probability these costs were met by the Allans themselves. In researching Nellie's story it has became increasingly apparent that her husband had independent means far beyond the income provided by a Free Church stipend.

Just a few years later, in 1886, the Allans bought the late 18th century Bayanne House and the crofting estate that went with it. Situated along the shore of Sella Firth (the bay on the east shore of Basta Voe) the Bayanne estate was made up of the slate-roofed Bayanne house and newly-adjoined schoolhouse, along with crofts and rigs that led down to the shore. Although this was probably as good crofting land as was in Sellafirth, it was no more than could provide a bare subsistence for the tenants' families. Rents from about seven crofts and Bayanne House with the newly-built schoolhouse were hardly a prime investment opportunity for the Allans. There had to be another reason for the purchase. What motivated Nellie to devote twenty-nine years of her life to the folk of North Yell and her Sellafirth tenants in particular?

To survive, the men in Shetland crofts needed employment in the haaf fishing, or away from home at the Greenland whaling or other dangers on the sea. Church ministers encouraged couples to marry young and have large families so to increase the labour force available to the merchant-lairds for the haaf fishing. For the women, the croft meant drudgery and bearing large families. There was still no security of tenure. Improvement of dwellings by tenants resulted in higher rents. I think the Gloup disaster would have shaken Nellie to the core. I don't believe she looked on it as a tragic act of God that the community could pick itself up from and carry on. I think Nellie saw the Gloup disaster as a consequence of the harsh crofting system and the conditions of uncertainty and poverty in which her parishioners endured.

Families of seven to twelve existing in two-roomed croft houses made conditions right for the spread of deadly tuberculosis. Conditions in overcrowded croft houses were less than sanitary, ideal conditions for the spreading of hepatitis. A young Nellie had seen two of her siblings die a lingering death from tuberculosis, now her youngest brother Bertie was dying from the disease (he succumbed in 1887). By purchasing the Bayanne estate she could start to make a difference to other families' sufferings by becoming a different kind of

---

7   Children of the Manse, Growing Up in Victorian Aberdeenshire. Alice Thiele Smith, Astrid Hess, Gordon K. Booth.
8   Obituary of James Hamilton Allan. Ecclegan, ministers of the Free Church of Scotland 1843-1900.
9   Ibid.

landowner. TB still hadn't finished with the Smith family, however. In 1894 her most famous brother, William (Will) Robertson Smith, friend, mentor and unfailing pillar of strength to her and her siblings, also died from the disease that had long bedevilled her family. He was just forty-eight years old.

Over the next thirteen years the Allans continued to live in the Sellafirth Manse, renting out the Bayanne house, school and crofts. The Bayanne estate was improved, old houses were renovated. Nellie had her hands full during this time. James seems to have been a mercurial character prone to fits of depression and taking to his bed, leaving Nellie to take the Church services, teach and fulfil much of the pastoral work. Anecdotal remarks made by my mother and folk of her generation in North Yell, even as late as 2004[10], confirm that James "had an eye for the ladies" and an illegitimate child was rumoured. All of which pretty much supported Nellie's sister's opinion of him.

James Hamilton Allan died suddenly of a hepatic ulcer in the Sellafirth Manse on 11th March, 1899. There is a granite plaque to his memory on the front of Sellafirth Free Kirk (later Church of Scotland and now a private house) which reads: *"The bell of this Church was erected by the congregation and friends to the Glory of God and in loving memory of Rev J.H. Allan who was faithful minister here from 1880 to 1899"*. The inventory of his personal estate (excluding Bayanne) shows it to be a mixture of bank deposits and investments amounting to £759 19s 8d (equal to £68,000 today). He'd left Nellie well provided for.

Following the death of her husband, Nellie moved into the house at Bayanne which was to become her home for the next ten years. She carried on managing and improving the estate. At least two new houses were built for her tenants: firstly the appropriately named Ladysmith (although probably named after the ending of the siege of Ladysmith, Natal in February 1900); next she had Allanbrae built sometime before 1909. Nellie continued to serve the folk of Sellafirth with pastoral care, teaching in the school and holding Bible classes.

Nellie loved Sellafirth and the folk loved her, but her health had never been the best and eventually she gave in to her siblings' desire to have her return to Scotland. She reluctantly left Shetland in 1909 and bought a house at Peterculter, near Aberdeen. She soon got involved in pastoral work there too, but kept on the Bayanne estate and rented out Bayanne House. From photographs of a ladylike Nellie and family recollections[11] the move seems to have given her, for the very first time, some well-deserved "me time" (in today's parlance). In early 1917 Nellie caught a lingering flu and died on the 17th of February of that year. From her obituary in a Shetland newspaper[12]: *"She would have graced the most select society in the land, but she elected to live and labour here, giving of her best for the good of all"*; *"Her heart was in Sellafirth, where she spent the best and happiest years of her life"*; *"Her tenants of Bayanne estate, mourn a kind and generous proprietor"*.

---

10   Astrid Hess. (pers.comm.).
11   Ibid.
12   Ibid.

Nellie Deans Allan; 1890s. Photo © Astrid Hess.

Nellie Allan's story is one of a close-knit family, happiness, tragedy, unrequited love and unstinting service to the community. Her efforts were much more than just appreciated, she was respected and loved for the twenty-nine years she lived in Sellafirth. Fifty years after she left Sellafirth she was still being remembered fondly by all who knew her. Her efforts in the community she served were still being recalled one hundred years after the Gloup disaster. She loved Sellafirth and dedicated so much of her life to the folk there yet she missed Keig, the manse and her family. Nellie wrote a poem in the Doric by which she remembers *The Dear Auld Hame*:

The Dear Auld Hame

Oh, the auld hame, the dear auld hame!
Close by the Kirk it stood,
Wi' ne'er anither hoose in sicht,
Embowered in a wood.
Sweet roses clustered the windows roun',
The ivy decked the wa';
An' roun' the door sweet briar we trained –
Fu' weel I min' it a'.

An ample yaird, weel stocked wi' flooers,
Berrybus' and shrub and tree
Lay roun' the hoose on ilka side;
A picture fair to see.
There ilka ane had an apple tree,
Ilk ane a garden plot;
Where grew sweet pinks an' violets,
An' blue forget-me-not.

'Twas fair, sae fair i' the bonnie Spring,
When the leaves were buddin' green,
The apple trees decked wi' clusters rare,
An' wi' bridal white the gean.
The beech hedge cast his auld broon coat,
Had keepit the frost awa',
An' trigged him oot in a bran' new suit,
The wonder of ane an' a'.

When lessons were dune, we roamed the woods,
I wat a merry ban',
An' the firstlin' o' each wild gem we laid
Wi' pride in oor mither's han'.
Oh, whiles in the quest o' a sair socht nest,

We gaed ower far astray;
But helter-skelter hame we raced,
At father's first "cooee."

In Simmer's prime 'twas fairer still,
Wi' mony a sheltered nook,
Where aft we sat in the leafy shade,
Wi' work or story book.
An' in evening hush, blackbird an' thrush,
Wi' music filled the air;
Ah me! I hear nae sangs like these
Sin' last I heard them there.

Maybe the birds still sing as sweet,
As sweet may blaw the flooers;
Maybe, maybe, but ah, they bloom
For ither han's than oors.
Nae mair the dear woods echo back
Oor lauchter an' oor sang;
Nor the auld hame ring wi' merry din,
When winter nichts are lang.

A stranger stands in father's place,
We hear his voice nae mair;
Sae powerfu' in the preachin', he,
Sae earnest in his prayer.
For he's won safe tae his far, far hame,
An' five o' us beside;
The circle's growing narrow noo,
That used to be sae wide.

Ah yes! love may keep out the cold,
As England's poet saith;
But it canna' snatch oor dear ones frae
Tha caul', caul' grip o' death:
But the love that's higher and wiser far
Than the best oor hearts have given,
Has gathered them safe – one day we'll be
An unbroken circle in heaven.

We're a' grown up and scattered noo,
Far frae the dear auld hame;
An' some ha'e risen till high place,
An' won a famous name;

But high or low, in foreign lands,
Or here or anywhere,
Nane o' us will forget oor hame,
Nor what we learned there.

Nellie Allan Smith.

Excursus 2:
The Devil's Own
– John Walker

Today you might call John Walker "a chancer" or "a con man"; he was certainly an unscrupulous manipulator of people and the law. In 1860s' and 1870s' Shetland he was nicknamed "the Director General of Shetland" for the ruthless total control he exerted over the tenants on his employer's estates. His disregard for the social upheaval and misery that implementing his vision for Shetland was causing made him the most hated man on the islands. Walker was Machiavellian to the core, my grandfather called him "da Deevil's own".

John Walker was born in Aberdeen in October 1835. His father was a linen weaver turned well-to-do businessman with a shop on Union Street. Walker dropped out of Aberdeen Grammar School aged fifteen. Two years later he was outward bound for Australia, landing in Melbourne in April 1853. Soon he was managing a gold-buying business and by age eighteen was managing an import/export business. He arrived in the new colony of Victoria in the gold rush days when law and order was practically nonexistent. He'd have seen life in the raw and how Aboriginals were treated worse than animals by the colonists. He'd have seen how the gold diggers' opposition and revolt over licence tax was bloodily crushed by the colonial forces in 1854. Perhaps this is where Walker got the idea that by treating native people with contempt and by manipulation of the law he could get the results he wanted.

Walker certainly wasn't a man to let the grass grow under his feet. In December 1854 he married Mary Ball Plummer, also aged 19. Three years and two daughters later they left Melbourne and returned to Aberdeen. Perhaps he thought the grass was greener back in Scotland? More likely his impulsive nature and powers of persuasive and manipulative argument had got him into trouble and he left Australia before some scores were settled.

Shetland through the first half of the 19th century saw great demographic changes. The population had increased dramatically from about 22,000 to 32,000. This was partially due to the control of smallpox, which would periodically wipe out twenty-five per cent of the population during the previous century. Land ownership had changed, with many landowners, now merchant-lairds, buying into the lucrative (for them) salt fish trade in a big way. Lairds provided the boats and the lines to their tenant-crofter/haaf-fishermen who in turn were required to sell fish caught to their merchant-laird. Prices of fish due to the tenants were set by the lairds, often set as a value against goods in their shops. This was the hated truck system whereby tenant crofters were tied to the "company store" by a vicious cycle of debt and credit. It took two major haaf fishing disasters, the hardships of the clearances and two parliamentary commissions of enquiry to get rid of it. Security of tenure for crofters only came through an act of parliament in 1886.

For the merchant-lairds more tenants equated to more haaf fishermen and more profit. In order to facilitate this, with the collusion of the church, marriage at a young age and large families were encouraged. To provide more tenanted crofts the best crofting land was subdivided into smaller units while sections of poorer scattald lands were acquired for prospective tenants to build a croft house and subsist on. Crofters built the houses on the new land themselves but had to pay rent on the house as well; and when they improved the house or the land the rent went up. This added to the increase of population and put a huge pressure on resources, particularly land. In poor fishing years crofters were in continual debt to the lairds; poor harvests brought famine in the hungry 1840s and 50s. There was no security of tenure; debt could see a family evicted. Sons of the crofter refusing to fish for the merchant-laird could mean a hefty fine for the tenant, or eviction, as could the sale of womenfolks' knitted goods to another merchant for better money. Poverty and hardship was endemic among crofters in mid-19th century Shetland.

If all this wasn't bad enough for the crofters, John Walker 'ebbed up' on Shetland's shores. By 1860 he was a tenant-farmer leasing a large (by Shetland standards) farm on Bressay from the Garth estate. By 1862 he'd built himself a large house on Bressay, called Maryfield after his wife. By 1866 he'd persuaded absentee laird Major Cameron of Garth that he could manage the estates of Garth and Annsbrae on his behalf and was appointed factor in that year. Over the next few years tenants not only suffered successive poor fishing and failed harvests, but endured a level of intimidation and evictions by Walker of a severity unprecedented in Shetland. Evictions of crofting communities to make sheep farms had of course happened before. Notably three-hundred people had been gradually cleared from the Nicolson estate on Fetlar between 1820 and 1850 leading to further overcrowding by subdivision of existing crofting land into tenancies elsewhere.

Walker saw Shetland in terms of tracts of underutilised land populated by indolent natives paying nominal rent to the lairds. He thought that he could make better use of the land and make estates more profitable. As in Australia, what was to happen to the natives was of little consequence. If he had control of the Garth estate he could set an example for others to follow, and make money. Walker's master plan was to turn the estate's crofting land into sheep farms. Not farms running the small native sheep, but flocks of larger breeds from mainland Scotland that would produce much larger lambs and more-profitable wool clips. For sheep farms to work, arable land growing the crofter's crops had to become grazing, so the crofters had to be moved off the land. The common grazing, the scattald, used communally by all the crofters, would also be needed for his sheep.

Walker was soon spending the estate's money on fencing material, fencing contractors, building sheep fanks, shepherds and houses for them, as well as stock. This was largely money borrowed by the estate from the government for land improvement, in this case a loan of £10,000[13] (equivalent to £800,000 today). He needed to see a return for the investment, and quickly. He couldn't afford long-term eviction and resettlement of his tenants, he needed them out as soon as possible. This he did by making living on the estate's crofts impossible. He drew up new rules for his tenants so that crofts were revalued at a higher rent that in poor fishing years they would be unable to meet. This involved the crofter having to follow a permanent improvement plan for the land by expansion and drainage that would increase rents and incur other charges. If the factor decided that the "improvements" weren't satisfactory the crofter's lease was terminated.

Walker's new rules banned crofters from use of the scattald, including the ebb, which all the crofters needed for day-to-day survival. The scattald provided peat for fuel, poans for roofing, nurseries for kale plants, as well as summer grazing for kye, sheep and 'grice'. Foreshore seaweed supplemented the diet of the animals, winter kelp provided manure for the rigs, and shell sand improved the land and was essential for poultry. If somehow a tenant could still manage to keep animals Walker had an answer for that too: they would have to seek the landlord or factor's permission to keep male breeding animals on the croft and they couldn't keep a dog. Some produce from the croft (even if there was a surplus) couldn't be sold. If some of the croft land was required for the landlord for some other purpose it could be taken and the size of the croft reduced.

Walker's scheme worked. Tenants who couldn't immediately accept the impossible new rules had to sign a document terminating their leases. Anyone trying to hang on and circumvent the rules found themselves in court. The suddenness of the new regime being imposed on them must have had the tenants reeling; to use a 20th century expression, it was "shock and awe". Heads of households now had the awful decision whether to try to survive the new regime or tear their families away from their homes and community for an uncertain future.

In reality there was no choice. Walker's rules and intimidation saw to that. At the mouth of Basta Voe in Yell, between 1867 and 1868, the crofting township of Burraness along with crofts at Kirkabister, Uncadal and Bigsetter, saw the

---

13 John Walker's Shetland. Wendy Gear. 2005. The Shetland Times Ltd.

evictions of: *"seventeen families, one hundred and two people with an average age of forty-five for the head of the household"*[14]; my great-great-grandfather Robert Nisbet and his family included. No attempt to re-home or assist these families was made by the Garth estate. Almost overnight a young, thriving community was uprooted and scattered. *"Twenty-eight of the children who lived there would be primary school age in the present day"*[15]. No one ever returned. The walls of the crofts still stand there, a stark testament to the arrogant beliefs of one man given his head by an absentee landlord.

Burraness, Yell. Cleared by John Walker.

Lumbister, Yell. Cleared by John Walker.

The same story was repeated again and again as crofts and townships emptied across the Garth estate lands on North Yell: Basta, Colvister, Volister, Lumbister, Wast-a-Firth and Vigon. The Garth lands in Unst and Delting suffered the same fate. Dozens of families were looking for new tenancies with no means of subsisting until they found somewhere. My great-grandfather, John Urquhart, was head of one of the three families, totalling thirty-one people, evicted from Lumbister. He was lucky; he found a tenancy in Basta. Robert Nisbet had to build

---

14 Ibid.
15 Ibid.

Author's great grandfather John Urquhart.

a temporary shelter out of 'poans' for his family in Cunnister until he found a place in Colvister. Many left Shetland never to return.

The weather in the years of eviction from 1867 to 1869 was appalling. Summer weather was cold and wet, grain didn't ripen and potatoes rotted in the fields. Dependent as they were on the produce of the field and sea, many were now in dire straits. The displaced found shelter with friends or relatives in crofts not owned by the Garth estate, leading to more overcrowding, misery and starvation. Walker's view of failed harvests was lack of effort: *"However incredible it may appear, many, indeed the generality of Shetlanders prefer idleness and semi-starvation to honest labour with its sweet reward"*[16]. Despite continued reports in the national press by visitors to Shetland of privation of the population, Walker continued to be in denial. He wrote letters to the contrary in newspapers stating that charity and relief was unnecessary. Not only that, he wrote to the Home Secretary and to the Shetland MP stating categorically that appeals to the government for charitable relief of destitution on Unst be rejected.

Resistance was useless, but resistance there was. Threats were made against Walker's life but none were carried out. In a small community the perpetrators would soon be discovered. Shetlanders have an unfortunate trait of not being able to stick together against authority; there would always be some willing to break ranks for personal gain. Three men did challenge Walker and a local employee as they were surveying Kirkabister crofts in 1867. Insults and threats of violence were exchanged. The upshot of this was that the men, including my great-grandfather Willie Gibby Nisbet, were charged with Breach of the Peace and Assault, found guilty and fined £1:1s each (equivalent to £80 each today). After that Walker carried a loaded revolver.

The reporting of this court case did however bring Walker's actions to a wider audience but to little avail. Absentee Major Cameron was alerted to Walker's doings but took little notice. As Walker's men erected fences to rail off the scattald, the offending fencing stakes and wire were burned and vandalised by the tenants of North Yell. Walker responded by letters threatening and blackmailing tenants in the area. Two young Anderson boys from Sellafirth were accused of overturning a barrel of tar used for preserving stakes. There was lack of evidence but Walker and Major Cameron wanted them made an example of as a deterrent to others. The boys were jailed in Fort Charlotte for six days.

In 1871 the tenants on the island of Bressay became Walker's next target and were subjected to his new rules of tenancy. There was a tenants' revolt. This seems to have been too close to home for Major Cameron and he was losing faith in his factor. Walker and family left Bressay for Aberdeen in 1872. Walker still kept his factorship for a few more years and was still heavily involved in Shetland affairs. Although now absent from Shetland he was elected to several school boards. Credit where credit is due; it was through Walker's efforts and battles with the government that there were greatly-improved school buildings and education in Shetland.

---

16 Ibid.

Author's great-grandfather, William Gilbert Nisbet.

The merchant-lairds who ran the truck system were unhappy with Walker's removal of folk from the isles. Less folk meant fewer crofter/fishermen to truck with. Walker opposed truck because this system of barter was a way of paying rent and keeping tenants on the land. Other than the merchant-lairds, only Lerwick lawyer William Sievwright seemed to vehemently oppose Walker by taking up crofters' cases. Walker was integrating and ingratiating himself with his new social class and in local politics, and he had the law on his side. It seems no other big estate owners or the great and the good of Lerwick were prepared to criticise or help oppose his actions. Perhaps they were waiting to see if his experiment in a form of local ethnic cleansing was going to benefit them. Many were happy to go into partnership with Walker in business ventures. The first of these was the Shetland Steam Company Ltd in which they bought shares to purchase a steam vessel for the North Isles route. In 1868 Walker was elected chairman of the company; the vessel they bought was the *Chieftain's Bride*, a vessel that proved to be unsuitable for the job but struggled on until the company was wound up in 1876.

He continued in his business ventures, some dubious. Chief among these was his involvement in chromite mining. On the island of Haaf Grunie there was a chromite quarry over which Walker had to fight and win a fraud case in 1875. The following year he was sued for withholding proceeds of chromite quarrying on Unst. His sharp practices were now getting him into trouble and Major Cameron was wanting rid of him. Other business ventures included a shareholding in the Shetland Fishing Company Ltd., of which he was a director by 1873. It owned a fleet of smacks fishing for cod in the waters of Iceland, Faeroe and Rockall. The company had a chequered history and went into liquidation in 1880. Another venture saw him lose money on a cargo of Shetland whale blubber that went rotten. It was his lease of the Sandlodge copper mine and its operation by his Sumburgh Mining Company from 1872 to 1880 that first bankrupted John Walker. His bankruptcy ended his business interests in Shetland.

Always the chancer 1881 saw John Walker plus family arrive in Cape Town, South Africa. He was now employed as an immigration agent to inspect vacant land with a view to recruit farmers from Scotland to settle there. Even in his recruiting material he seems to have been economical with the truth regarding the promises of a new life in South Africa. Always the con man he claimed he knew about building railways and won a contract in 1884 to build forty-two miles of railway line. His company only managed to construct seven miles. This ran into financial trouble and became known as "Walker's folly". Another Walker company, the Grand Junction Railway, went bust in 1889 and protracted legal battles followed. Following that he built more railway lines, fought more protracted court battles, lost other people's money and eventually returned to Britain in 1899. He first stayed in Putney, where he got involved in local politics. His long-suffering wife Mary, bearer of fifteen children, died there in 1903. Walker occasionally visited Shetland, still friends with the great and the good. He returned to Aberdeen to live and died there, aged 81, in 1916.

In Edwardian times obituaries were generally glowing and the bad bits glossed over. It surely is a measure of the "da Deevil's own" that extracts from John Walker's obituary reads thus: *"What others had failed to do by persistent effort extending over a long period, he accomplished in a very short time by sheer force of character. Crofters were evicted by the score, and many acres which had furnished the means of livelihood to numerous families were conveyed into sheep runs, and the people turned out 'to sink or swim'. His views upon the land question were extreme, even for his day, and in his desire to promote what he considered 'the right' he allowed nothing to stand in his way... He seemed to harbour the idea that despite climatic conditions and poverty of soil he could raise the standard of agriculture and stock raising in Shetland quite as high as it was in Aberdeenshire. He failed in this, as he was bound to do, but before he left the islands, many a smiling township was represented by the falling remnants of houses and office-houses, with the inhabitants scattered to the four winds."*[17]

---

17 *The Shetland Times*, 20th June 1917.

Excursus 3: Da Gulsa Shall and da Trowie Kapp

One of my earliest memories of growing up in Sellafirth is sitting by the big open fire in the Wasterhoose but-end when the subject of the "da Gulsa Shall" (shell) came up in conversation; perhaps it was a night when neighbours had come along for a yarn long before the days of 'Yell for light' and TV.

The first object was a kapp (wooden bowl), about thirteen centimetres across, inside which lay a much smaller concave 'shell-like' object. These were "da Gulsa Shall" and the "da Trowie Kapp". Both objects were passed around, and my mother would recount what she knew of the story. There was also much speculation as to what the shall had been before it had been found by my great-great-grandmother, Catherine Nisbet. Then, and again in later years, I had heard of the shall being described (erroneously as it turns out) as being part of a person's knee-cap.

Catherine Nisbet (née Donaldson) was the second wife of Robert Nisbet and, between her marriage in 1843 and being cleared in 1868, lived with him at their croft at Uncadal, near The Daal of Kirkabister, Yell. The story as far as could be remembered was that one of Catherine's eight children (all born between 1843 and 1857) was ill with gulsa (jaundice). Catherine had dreamt that if she went to a 'trowie-knowe' (probably in Djupidaal, between Sellafirth and Cunnister) she would find a shall that would provide a cure for the bairn's gulsa. She was to draw water from a place where the runoff from three proprietors' land met and cause the bairn to drink the water from the shall. The hand-carved wooden kapp that accompanies the shall was used for holding the water. How the kapp and the shall came to be together or the exact ritual of their use had not survived the telling down to my mother's generation, but a version of the story is recorded in *Shetland Traditional Lore* by Jessie M.E. Saxby.

Gulsa Shell and Trowie Kapp

Author's great-great grandmother Catherine Nisbet (née Donaldson).

Uncadal, Daal o' Kirkabister, Yell. Home of Catherine and Robert Nisbet.

Extracts from *Shetland Traditional Lore* by Jessie M.E. Saxby (Grant & Murray, Edinburgh, 1932.)
Page 151 to 152:

One night a family having gone to bed, heard a noise in the "but end o' da hoose", and the house mother peeped through a chink and saw a number of trows at the fire nursing a sick one. She heard them say that their invalid was afflicted with jaundice, and they were pouring water on her out of a small wooden bowl (known in Shetland as a Kapp).

As they poured they said, "This is the wey to cure."

The woman instantly fixed her eyes upon the kapp, and called out, "The blessing o' the Lord be aboot yon kapp." The trows instantly disappeared, leaving the kapp, which was kept in that family and lent to persons suffering from jaundice.

Once a man dreamt that if he went to a certain spot among the cliffs he would there find a shell that would cure the jaundice if he would use it as directed.
He went to the place and found the shell. It was formed of bone, smooth inside, and resembled a man's knee-cap. A Trow came to him and told him to use it along with the Trow-kapp. Further directions were as follows: The patient must go fasting and speech-less to a well flowing east. The person who accompanies the patient must carry the kapp, inside of which must rest the shell. The kapp must be gently dropped on the water, and allowed to fill itself as it gradually sinks. When full it must be lifted out, and some of the water in the shell must be sipped by the patient. Then the region of the heart and top of the head are sprinkled, and the remaining water in the shell is thrown high over the patient's head to fall upon the ground.

This performance is repeated three times. No words must be spoken until the patient and friend return home. Then the person who officiated says: "I hae used the means: Lord pit in the blessin'," and the patient must add Amen!

Page 160:

My nurse told me that when she was a child she suffered from jaundice, so her father borrowed the Trow-kapp and shell and used them in her behalf.

He paid a shilling, and she was cured after a fortnight's application of the cure.

How the Shall and the Kapp were passed on

Major Cameron's factor John Walker cleared Catherine and the family from the Uncadal croft in the 1868. They made a temporary shelter by building a 'feally-hoose' on the croft at Da Banks, Cunnister, tenanted by her son Willy Gibby Nisbet. From there they moved across Basta Voe to Colvister where they lived for about twenty years. By 1891 Catherine and husband Robert were back at Da Banks, living with their eldest son Willie Gibby, his family, his in-laws and his niece (14 in all). Robert died in 1902, aged 88, and Catherine in 1903, aged 86.

The Gulsa Shall and kapp were passed on to Catherine's grand-daughter Janet Nisbet (Willy Gibby's eldest daughter). The shell was often borrowed for use around North Yell; Janet is quoted as having to walk from Cunnister to North Yell for return of the shell. Last known use as an attempted cure was on Kitty Tulloch, living in the Old Schoolhouse, Sellafirth, Yell, around the time her daughter Maggie Tulloch was born in 1912. Kitty died soon after from TB.

When Janet left Shetland to work in service, the shall and the kapp were passed on to her sister Ellen Deans Allan Nisbet (my grandmother) then to her daughter, Ann Jessie Urquhart (my mother).

On the nature of the 'Gulsa Shall'

From her description of the objects and their borrowed usage I'm pretty sure that the shell and kapp Saxby was writing about was none other than the Gulsa Shall and Trowie Kapp in our possession. Although Saxby also describes the shell as resembling a man's knee-cap, it is obviously not a patella, for a human patella is circular-triangular bone and not deeply convex. Having said that though, it is easy to see from its overall shape and odd texture how it could be easily imagined by the layperson that this was a knee-cap.

Close examination of the shell, and comparison with a borrowed disc of the same material, shows that it was originally a flat, round disk of cartilage (not bone) from the spine of a small cetacean. It is likely that the Gulsa Shall was a disk that has been softened by boiling then pressed in a mould into the shape of the bowl of a spoon. This could have been done in the same way as which horn spoons used to be made in Shetland.

The story of da Gulsa Shall and da Trowie Kapp is a unique part of Shetland's folklore and both these objects are on permanent display in the Shetland Museum in Lerwick, in memory of my late mother Ann Jessie Fraser (née Urquhart).

Excursus 4: TripAdvisor Reviews

My thanks to all my guests who posted these kind comments on TripAdvisor.

"Good day out."
Reviewed 25 January 2013.
Had a day trip to Eshaness and that area with Allen Fraser and really enjoyed myself. Allen is very knowledgeable and chatty. He told me lots of interesting things about the geology of Eshaness and other things and even showed me the *Shetland Elephant*. He went at my (slow) pace and looked after me well and changed the tour a bit to cover all my interests and to work round the weather. I was on my own so changing things and taking it slowly worked well. Had a great day and hoping to do more trips with Shetland Geotours this year.

"Faultless day out in the far north of Shetland."
Reviewed 27 June 2013.
10 hours plus on a tour with a very knowledgeable guide called Alan from Lerwick to Unst. Perfectly timed with the ferries, beautiful barely accessible places and loads of local knowledge made this an unforgettable day. We were going to drive. So glad we didn't. Highly recommended!

"Fascinating and Wonderful Experience."
Reviewed 10 February 2014.
We were fortunate enough to spend two days with Allen when we booked a WildAbout Orkney tour of the Orkney and Shetland islands. Allen was our guide for our tour of Shetland. The two days were completely wonderful. Personally, I'm not all that interested in geology, but I found what Allen told us to be fascinating. He also was full of stories of the history, traditions, and every possible aspect of Shetland life. We even learned stories of his own family-

-like how his mother worked to gut fish at the rate of 40-60 a minute. I add this to say don't let the "Geotour" name make you shy from this experience. He was patient with our (sometimes ignorant) questions and was willing to accommodate special requests. For example, my husband is an equine veterinarian, so seeing the Shetland ponies was fun for us. Allen stopped the van so I could actually pet a particularly friendly one that came to my window. Another couple on our tour was interested in the Shetland Bus (something we had never heard of), and Allen detoured into Scalloway to show us the monument and explain its history. We never felt rushed and had ample time to explore areas, soak up the scenery, and talk with locals. He also suggested we read Ann Cleeves books set in the Shetland Islands, which we have thoroughly enjoyed. In fact, they may just encourage us to make a return trip. We can't recommend Allen highly enough. Visited September 2013.

"Amazing experience."
Reviewed 6 July 2014.
Joined Allen for 3 days exploring the main parts of the Shetland islands. He was so knowledgeable about geology, archaeology, history & culture of the islands; plus the huge variety of wildlife. This was my first visit to the islands and Allen made it so very interesting. Visited July 2014.

"A good Shetland Introduction."
Reviewed 26 July 2014.
A fair bit of travelling but it's a must on Shetland. Allen showed us a good variety of locations to explain the geological, historical and social aspects of this beautiful group of isles. If not for Allen I doubt we would have visited or covered the different areas covered. Well worth it in my view. Visited July 2014.

"Great overview of South Shetland."
Reviewed 9 August 2014.
When we got off our cruise ship tender, Allen and the Shetland Geotours van was waiting for us on the dock. Allen gave us a great overview of South Shetland, visiting St. Ninian's Isle, the Jarlshof ruins, Sumburgh Head bird reserve (to see Puffins), the Shetland Croft House museum, and Shetland Ponies. Allen was a knowledgeable guide and packed in so much during our tour. The van only fits 8 people, so you're guaranteed a nice small group size. Visited July 2014.

"Awesome Day!!"
Reviewed 17 August 2014.
We had a great day with Allen from Shetland Geotours. He met us at the dock in Lerwick. It was so easy. It was just my husband and I so we sat in the front seat with Allen. He took us all around the island. Such a beautiful place!! He is so knowledgeable about the area and gave us so much information about the geology and history. He ran met some people he knew and we got to hear him

speak Gallic *(sic)*. Midway we stopped at this nice little coffee shop where he knew the owner and we had some local specialties. At the end of the day he brought us right back to the pier. We had spent the whole day with Allen. It was a great experience and well worth the cost. I love the Shetland Islands! Well worth the visit. Visited June 2014.

"Fantastic day at Eshaness."
Reviewed 19 August 2014.
I went with Allen Fraser on a 'Geotour' to Eshaness when I was on holiday in August this year. I originally come from Shetland so was really doing the tour because I had a friend who had never been to Shetland before. I can't say how glad I am that I did the tour. I always knew that Shetland has an interesting geology, but had no idea just quite how interesting. Allen made the rocks come alive and what he doesn't know about the geology of Shetland isn't worth knowing. He picked us up from our accommodation in Lerwick, picked up a few more people, and off we went. He stopped at various points on the way up to Eshaness to point out features. We did the coast to coast walk, walking from the North Sea to the Atlantic Ocean (it's about 80 metres), at the Mavis Grind, the narrowest point on Shetland. After a very good lunch at the Breiwick Cafe in Eshaness, we set off to the Grind o' da Navir, a walk of about 1.5 hours taking it slowly. Eshaness has one of the most spectacular coasts in Shetland and the weather was amazing, but, best of all, Allen kept up a commentary about the rock formations of the cliffs and the different types of rock. I never knew that Eshaness used to be a huge volcano and millions of years ago was 30 degrees south of the Equator. The Grind is an amazing place (shown on Coast), and if you are able I would urge you to do this tour. I took some fairly good photos which are attached, but they don't really do the place justice. It's more than just a geology tour, though. Get Allen to take you to the graveyard at Eshaness to see the grave of Johnnie 'Notions' who came up with a vaccination for smallpox before Jenner did, or the grave of Donald Robertson who was killed by 'the stupidity of Lawrence Tulloch .... who sold him nitre instead of Epsom salts'. As I said, I used to live in Shetland, but am really glad I decided to go on this tour with Allen. His knowledge is second to none and is matched only by his enthusiasm for his subject and for Shetland generally. I can't recommend this tour too highly.

"Fantastic tour."
Reviewed 22 October 2014.
We had a group of 16 from the NCL Star that took Shetland Geotours. Allen and James (*Island Trails*) were our guides. They were excellent. We were in two small buses with 8 in each bus. We learned much of the history, culture, economics and geology of the Shetlands. Also, we found the Shetlands to be a hidden gem. It was scenic and our lunch was five GBP each with great soup and sandwiches. Visited September 2014.

"Do Not Miss This!"
Reviewed 11 May 2015.
I planned my entire trip to Shetland around Allen Fraser's hike to Eshaness, so my expectations were pretty high. Harrumphs – they weren't nearly high enough; he delivered, and delivered, and delivered! Before beginning our hike, Allen stopped the van at Mavis Grind, where the Atlantic Ocean is just a stone toss from the North Sea. Seeing that interesting geography was everything I had expected, but then he showed us an exhibit of geologically-significant rocks that he had helped design. As he talked about the rocks, our small group slowly began seeing the very ground beneath our feet as a fascinating piece of Earth's history. Back in the van, he told us the stories and legends of the places we passed, all the while keeping an eye on the notorious Shetland weather. When he noticed rain in the distance, he took us to Ronas Hill to climb around and over boulders of red granite until the rain over Eshaness had cleared.

Somewhere along the hike to Eshaness, along the heart-stopping cliffs, gloriously green grass, swooping seabirds, and thunder of the waves, I fell madly in love with Shetland. My teenage son did, too – especially after he discovered puffins watching him from a crevasse. Allen showed us rocks that storm waves had thrown far into the pasture, patiently taught us how to recognize different minerals in the rocks, and opened our eyes to a world we had looked at but never before seen. Not to pressure Shetland Geotours or anything, but whatever expectations you have for this tour – double them!

"We visited and learnt so much."
Reviewed 24 May 2015.
During our week based in Lerwick we booked 3 tours with Allen, South Mainland history, archaeology tour & puffins, Scalloway, Brochs & Mousa guided walk and finally Eshaness tour & guided walk. It would have been difficult to have found a better way to get such a detailed look at different parts of Mainland. It was also very useful being picked up at our accommodation as we were staying on the edge of Lerwick. Three great days out. Thank you Allen. Visited May 2015.

"Slow and steady."
Reviewed 1 July 2015.
My day with Alan Fraser started in the best way possible: he rearranged the start of the tour to make sure I could get to the 5:30 ferry easily. How perfect is that?! I met Alan at the tourist information centre in Lerwick, and he stowed my bag in the trunk of the van, then went to pick up the others on our tour. He was thoughtful, informative, and deliberate all day. We had lunch in Braewick as a group, went to all sorts of lovely, out-of-the-way spots, and I even got to pet a Shetland pony! Then he dropped me at the ferry on his way back into town. A simple and pleasurable way to spend a day! Visited June 2015.

"Fantastic value."
Reviewed 20 July 2015.
A very busy enjoyable day. We travelled all round the south mainland and saw seals, puffins etc. The visit to Jarlshof was extremely interesting and knocks spots of Skara Brae in the Orkneys. Lovely to be driven by someone who knows the area and is so knowledgeable. Recommended. Visited June 2015.

"Excellent way to see some of Shetland and its geology."
Reviewed 21 July 2015.
According to Allen Fraser, this season is your last to take a tour with him (another geologist is expected to take over). But a day with this guide is so informative and possibly dramatic that I'd recommend it highly. My tour went to a number of sites, but chiefly Esha Ness on a day of strong winds that provided a glimpse of the forces that continue to shape Shetland. It was wonderful. Visited May 2015.

"Spectacular Scenery, Professional and Friendly Guide."
Reviewed 22 July 2015.
We booked a day-long tour with Alan Fraser of Shetland Geotours during our June cruise stop with Holland America. When we left the ship that was the last time we saw a motor coach and the usual tour crowd. Instead, we boarded Alan's comfortable van and he treated us to a tour of the North Mainland. Among the stops were Brae; Mavis Grind; Ronas Hill; Braewick Café; Esha Ness Cliffs; and the Tangwick Haa Museum. With the van, we were able to drive the single-track roads where motor coaches can't travel. Alan provided excellent commentary on the culture, history and life in the Shetlands, and he answered all questions in a friendly and easy manner. He booked lunch at a local restaurant far away from town, where we enjoyed wonderful sandwiches and the incredible warm carrot soup. Frankly, when we booked this cruise, we had low expectations for Lerwick and the Shetlands. With Alan as our guide, this became one of our favourite ports. Visited June 2015.

"Very friendly and knowledgeable guide."
Reviewed 18 August 2015.
Mr. Fraser had a tour for our cruise ship. We visited the area of Voe and Brae which is north of Lerwick where we landed. The bus had 8 people on board I felt we got individual treatment. The area we drove round was very barren and reminded me a lot of the Yorkshire Dales. Mr. Fraser is very knowledgeable about geology and told us of the rocks in the area. There were a lot of sheep on the island which did outnumber the people. We also got to see a Scottish Highland cow with its young. Unfortunately it was windy and rainy and made for a cold trip depending on which bit of the island we were on. We stopped for lunch at a local café. Visited July 2015.

"Tour of South Mainland."
Reviewed 30 August 2015.
We had a great day out with Allen visiting the South Mainland. Everywhere he took us was interesting, and his friendly and informative commentary made the day most enjoyable. The highlights of the day for us were St Ninian's Isle and the bird sanctuary at the southern tip of the mainland, where we took some fantastic puffin photos. Visited June 2015.

Glossary

Here you will find dialect words that I have introduced in the text. Shetland dialect words, once in everyday use on the croft and in the boat, are increasingly becoming confined to the sarcophagus of the dictionary.

It is probably fair to say that our native tongue will live on for a time by the efforts of its champions and by students of poetry and prose. Placenames will be the last vestiges of our Norn language to die, but here too there is dilution by the use of anglicised versions of Shetland place-names on maps and road signs. Anglicised spellings falsify the true pronunciation so that over time the original meanings that record a vital part of our history become lost. Today, when most school teachers are non-dialect speakers, dialect poetry and prose is only now appearing in some parts of the curriculum. Too little too late I fear, as the essence of the spoken word is becoming lost. Our dialect will survive on the written page, but sadly, not on the tongue. Future students of our dialect will be members of a dead poets' society.

A

aalie - mollycoddle. Aalie-lambs were female lambs that were kept over winter and intended for next year's breeding stock. These were well fed and kept inside at night in the 'lamhoose'.
aert - Earth.
aeshins - the space between the roof and the top of the inside wall of a building.
andoo - row very slowly.
antrin - occasional.
atween - between.

B

baal - throw.
baa - large isolated sunken rock.
banks-broo - edge of the cliffs above the shore.

bearin – drifting of snow.
ben-end – bedroom and/or best room of a croft house.
biggit-in – built-in in the sense of making an opening smaller.
bonxie – the Great Skua.
braand-iron – griddle.
broch – Circular tower of drystone construction from the Iron Age (~ 300 BC to 200 AD).
brods – boards of a book.
Broo – The Department of Health and Social Security. The term originated as a Glasgow pronunciation of bureau as in Employment Bureau, a former name for this institution.
birze – squeeze.
BMB – The company British Motor Boats who also designed a two-wheeled tractor (BMB Cultmate) that was manufactured by the Brockhouse company of Southport.
buggi-flay – skinning a sheep while keeping the skin intact.
but-end – living room of a croft house.
byock – almost vomit.

C

caa – round up sheep on the common grazing.
cast yowes – ewes too old for breeding and fattened during the summer for killing in the autumn.
casting – cutting of peat using a 'tushker'.
clippins – small cuttings.
clootie-dugs – cloth sheepdogs; apparel waved at sheep during a caa.
coarn – generic term for a crop of barley and/or oats.
cole – small, cone-shaped haystack, covered and kept in place with redundant, cut up fishing nets.
colls – partially burned peats in the open fire.
Condor moment – a 1980s advert for enjoying Condor pipe tobacco.
craigs – rocks favoured for fishing from the shore.
craig-steen – jutting out rock on the foreshore overhanging the water, even at low tide.
crö – sheep pen.
croft – smallholding, traditionally a rented subsistence form of farming.
crofting act – the Crofters Holdings (Scotland) Act of 1886 is an Act of the Parliament of the United Kingdom that created legal definitions of the crofting parish and crofter, and for the first time granted security of land tenure to crofters. This act broke the power of the landlords and allowed for improvement of housing.
crofting toonships – a group of crofts established on better land (inbye) sharing a large area of poorer-quality hill grazing (scattald) for their livestock.

D

da – the (definite article)
day's work – community effort whereby neighbours would give a day's work on each other's croft in return for the same.
dee – (pronoun) second person singular, used in a familiar sense.
dek – wall.
dell – to dig over ground with a spade.
denner – mid-day meal.
dess – haystack built in the yard for winter animal fodder.
dipplin-tree – similar to a dibble, a long, pointed wooden pole with a t-bar top for poking holes in the soil to plant potatoes.
dorro – a fishing line wound onto a board used for handlining with a weight and feathered or baited hooks.
dratsi – otter. Shetland otters are not sea otters as often supposed but European freshwater otters, possibly introduced by Norse settlers as a source of fur.
du – (pronoun) familiar form of you.

E

ebb – the shore between low and high water marks.
eela – sea fishing; traditionally from crofters own small boat using a hand line.

F

faa (also faw) – sheep's intestines some of which were used as a bags for cooking.
fan – snowdrift (noun); found (verb).
flaying – flensing. Paet-banks would be flayed by removing the top foot or so of turf, i.e. the surface-growing layer, which was placed in the space left by the previous year's peat cutting, so preserving the peat-forming layer.
feally-hoose – a shelter constructed from turf.
flit – to move.
foweraereen – traditional double-ended, four-oared open boat.
funs – collective enjoyment.
fur – ploughed furrow.

G

gather – bring together sheep on a defined area of the common grazing.
geng aff – go off fishing in a boat.
grice – pig.
grind – gate.
guized-up – in fancy dress.
gulsa – jaundice.

H

haaf-fishing – fishing in deep water by long-lines from six-oared open boats called sixaereen, often 30 to 40 miles offshore.
haddin oot a langer – passing the time.
haep – to weed and pile up earth around growing root crops using a hoe.
haet – heat.
hailed – pulled on board.
hairst – autumn, harvest-time.
hame-aboot – about home.
hap – knitted shawl.
hawnd-idle – hand-idle. Impulse always to be working at something even when sitting down; usually hand knitting.
hay-rig – hay-field.
hefting – management of sheep on large areas of communal grazing without shepherding. In the distant past sheep had to be kept within an unfenced area of hill land by constant shepherding. As successive generations of sheep are born on this land they learn the boundaries of their grazing. Over time this became an instinct to be passed from ewe to lamb over succeeding generations.
hentin – gathering up.
hill-folk – mythical dwellers in the hills; perhaps analogous to the hidden people of Faeroe or huldufólk of Iceland.
hirded – gathered together crops in the hairst.
home-kill – sheep from the croft killed and butchered for family consumption.
hömin – evening twilight.
horse-gook – snipe.
hurl – wheelbarrow.
hurling – using a wheelbarrow.

I

in-bye – fenced grazing land.

K

kapp – small hand-carved wooden bowl.
keel – Shetland pronunciation of kale.
keel-yerd – (aka planti-crö) a drystone-walled enclosure for growing Shetland kale, an old variety of cabbage.
kirn – butter churn.
klocks – beetles.
knapp – pretentious use of Queen's English.
knave – fist.
kollie – home made oil lamp.
kye – cows.

L

lamhoose – lamb-house. An outbuilding where lambs are kept in winter.
leet – heed.
lempit – limpet.
link steens – stones attached by a loop of rope to weigh down fishing nets or roof thatch.
lowin – blazing.
Lukki's oo – bog cotton. Also known as Lukkimeeni's oo.

M

maa – herring gull.
mareel – marine phosphorescence due to planktonic marine organisms responding to mechanical disturbance of the water by emitting brief bright light.
meedoo – meadow.
meid – a fishing mark at sea found by taking visual cross-bearings of prominent features on the land.
misanter – misadventure.

N

neep – turnip, usually called swede in England. Grown in Shetland since the 18th century.
neesick – porpoise.
nev-foo – fist-full.
noost – boat-shaped, man-made hollow well above the high water mark and the beach where a boat is kept when not in use.

P

paets – blocks of peat cut and dried for fuel.
paet-bank – the cutting where peat was extracted.
paet-casting – cutting peat blocks from a paet-bank using a 'tushker'.
paet-hill – an area on the 'scattald' designated for peat cutting.
paet-raising – lifting cut peat off the ground and gathering to form small pyramids.
paet-rooging – amalgamating small pyramids to form larger ones.
paet-reek – peat smoke.
paet-right – each croft with grazing rights on the scattald had the 'right' to cut peat for their own use. The grazing on the scattald and peat-rights were administered by the Grazing Constable; a local crofter appointed to the job.
paet-stack – peat stack.

paet-turning – once paets had been 'raised' for a week or so each paet would be turned around to enhance drying.
peenies – aprons.
peerie – small.
peerie-scarf – shag.
picters – pictures, cinema.
piltick – coalfish.
planticrub – a small circular stone-walled enclosure for growing Shetland kale-plants from seed which were then transplanted into larger kale-yards.
poans – large squares of turf.
pock-net – a long-handled net for catching sillicks attracted by soe.
punded – enclosed in sheep pens.

R

redd – used generally with up; e.g. tidy up, also recount genealogical connections.
reestit – salted and dried in peat smoke.
restin-shair – resting-chair. A long wooden bench-seat with a back and arms at either end.
rig – field.
rinner – narrow balk of wood along the wall used as a shelf.

S

saat-tub – wooden tub or barrel containing salt brine.
sae – wooden tub with handles, traditionally used for washing clothes.
sailing – Shetlanders term for employment in the Mercantile Marine and Merchant Navy.
scarf – cormorant.
scattald – common open pasture for grazing, usually hills above arable croft land.
scrime – just able to see features by peering.
seggies – yellow iris.
seine-net – a shallow net set in a circle on the bottom and closed by towing.
selkie – seal.
shalder – the oyster catcher.
Shetland spade – a type of long-handled spade unique to Shetland.
Shetland keel – an old variety of cabbage grown in Shetland since at least the 17th century. This traditional crop was the only winter green vegetable available for both human and croft animals. It had the quality of high salt and frost resistance and would remain green all winter in the kale-yard where it could be accessed for daily use.
shimley – chimney.
shoormal – where waves break on the shore.
sillick – immature coalfish.
simmer – summer.

simmer-dim – summer night-time twilight between mid-May and mid-July.
sixaereen – six-oared, double-ended open boat.
skorie – immature herring gull.
skrövelings – small coarn (oats or barley) ricks built from sheaves.
skroo – large rick of coarn sheaves built in the yard for winter animal fodder.
smisslen - sand-gaper (shellfish).
snaa-böl – snow shelter for sheep.
soe – mashed limpets used as bait to attract sillicks.
soe-pot – a bowl-shaped depression cut in the craig-saet that acts as a mortar for mashing limpets.
Sparks – marine radio officer.
spoots – razor-clams.
sproot – to propel a spray outwards from the mouth.
stave kirn – plunge churn. Churning was done by a vertical, twisting movement of a long-handled plunger in a tall churn.
steamer's store – cargo shed for the MV *Earl of Zetland*; the small cargo vessel that plied between Lerwick and the North Isles of Shetland until the introduction of inter-island car ferries.
steen-biggit – stone built. The walls of Shetland croft houses were of dry stone construction.
steekit-stumnaa – thick sea-fog.
stook – sheaves of 'coarn' stood on end together in the field.
sungaets – with the direction of the sun's movement, clockwise.
swaar – swathe of hay or 'coarn' cut by a scythe.
swee – sting.
swill – wooden swivel for an animal's tether.

T

tang – seaweeds.
tawtees – (*Yell pronunciation*) potatoes. Only grown in Shetland as a crop since the 18th century.
tawtee-crö – an enclosure, often made from driftwood, in a dark corner of the barn where potatoes were stored.
tickets – slang for Merchant Navy officers certificates of competence.
tidder – the other.
trams – shafts, such as in a horse-drawn cart, wheel barrow, or two-wheeled tractor.
trial-bred – bred from a collie line with a good competition record in sheepdog trials.
troot – trout.
trootin – fishing for trout.
trowe – through.
trowie-knowe – hillock, knoll or mound said to be the entrance to where trows live.

trows – small mischievous mound dwellers in Shetland hills; analogous to Irish leprechauns.
truck – an arrangement in which employees are paid in commodities or some currency substitute in the employer's shop; restricted to certain commodities to benefit the employer.
tushker – a long-handled spade with a right-angled blade used for peat cutting.
twallin da coo – milking the cow at midday.
tystie – black guillemot.

U

uncan – unfamiliar.

V

vaege – journey.
voar – agricultural springtime.
voe – long narrow inlets from the sea in Shetland. These were pre-glacial valleys drowned by progressive sea level rise since the end of the last glaciation.

W

waar – broad-leaved kelp plants.
wark – job; work.
water-scheme – an initiative by the post-war ZCC to connect every home in Shetland to a public water supply.
wharve – turn and aerate 'swaars' of mown hay with a rake.
whitrit – stoat.
widdergaets – against the direction of movement of the sun, anticlockwise.
wilt – having lost all sense of direction.
wirkin – working.
wis – us.
wrack-wid – wreck wood.
wylks – whelks.

Y

yerd-dek – yard wall, usually around keel-yerd.
yoag – large horse mussel (*Modiolus modiolus*).
yoag-dreg – multi-pronged dredge towed over the sea bed to dislodge and capture large horse mussels.

Z

ZCC – Zetland County Council reorganised in 1975 along with Lerwick Town Council to become the present day Shetland Islands Council (SIC).